# CRICKET
## *An Illustrated History*

# CRICKET
## An Illustrated History

David Rayvern Allen

Phaidon · Oxford

Phaidon Press Limited,
Musterlin House,
Jordan Hill Road,
Oxford OX2 8DP

First published 1990

A CIP catalogue for this book is available from the British Library

ISBN 0 7148 2573 5

Typeset in England by BAS Printers Limited, Over Wallop, Hampshire
Printed and bound in Great Britain by William Clowes
Limited, Beccles and London

Picture research by Liz Sherriff
Design by Krystyna Hewitt

Captions to opening illustrations

(p.1) W.G. Grace as opener.

(p.2) An illustration from *The Windsor* magazine, taken from *Vanity Fair*. Wynyard played for
England, and also appeared for the Old Carthusians in their winning F.A. Cup Final team of 1881;
he also performed creditably as a figure skater.

(p.3) A three-dimensional pop-up Christmas card.

(p.5) The last word. R.M. Alexander's sketch showing the humbling of mere man, reproduced in
the pages of Victoriana.

(pp.6–7) An encounter at Menston in Yorkshire.

(p.8) A child playing cricket makes a potent brew for advertisers.

The title page for each chapter shows a chalk drawing by Albert Chevallier Tayler (1862–1925);
Ch. 1: A.E. Trott, Ch. 2: J.T. Tyldesley, Ch. 3: W. Rhodes, Ch. 4: S.M.J. Woods, and Ch. 5:
A.R. Warren. See also front cover.

**Acknowledgements**
The author would like to acknowledge the valued assistance of the following who helped in many different ways
during the preparation of this volume: Neil Drury, Liz Sherriff, Krystyna Hewitt, John Arlott, Graham Collyer,
David Cripps, Count Andre D'Aquino, David Frith, Stephen Green, John McKenzie, Nicholas Potter, Robert
Brooke and Peyton Skipwith.

**Photographic Acknowledgments**

D. Rayvern Allen: 3, 5, 8, 55 (top), 62, 67, 74, 75, 89, 106, 107, 110, 146, 158, 160;   Allsport: 32 (left), 41,
44 (top & bottom), 48, 66 (all except bottom centre), 77 (top) 80 (left), 90–1, 93, 99 (bottom), 100, 116;   Allsport/
Adrian Murrell: 34 (right), 52, 79, 97 (top), 114, 117, 126, 151, 157;   Allsport/Bob Martin: 150;   Count André
D'Aquino: 101 (top), 129, 136;   John Arlott: 118–19;   Bodleian Library: 13;   Bridgeman Art Library: 2, 15,
31 (bottom), 36, 38–9, 46–7, 58, 59, 103 (bottom), 111, 138–39, 139 (bottom);   Bridgeman Art Library/MCC:
10–11, 11 (bottom), 18–19, 28, 30–31, 42, 43, 51, 63, 86, 87, 96, 130–1, 152 (top), 162–3;   Burlington Galleries:
34 (left), 65 (bottom), 88 (left);   Burlington Galleries (Punch): 82–3;   Howard Carter/Crane Calman Gallery:
147;   Christie's: 12, 37, 65 (top), 84 (bottom), 148;   City of Westminster Archives: 29;   Graham Clarke:
26;   Courtauld Institute of Art/Knowle Estates: 20;   David Cripps: 1, 14, 23, 24, 50, 55 (centre and bottom),
60, 69, 72, 73, 81a, 88 (right), 98, 99 (top), 108, 113, 125, 144 (top), 156;   Nick Daly: 35; Judith Dobie: 128,
129;   Patrick Eagar: 6–7, 115, 122, 123, 132, 134, 135, 149 (bottom), 152–3 (bottom), 153 (right), 154,
155;   E.T. Archive: 57;   Mary Evans: 40, 45, 64, 66 (bottom centre), 68, 70, 71, 77 (bottom), 81b, 94, 95,
121, 124, 133;   David Frith: 145;   Susan Griggs Agency/Michael St Maur Sheil: 127;   Kathryn Jackson: 147
(bottom); Tony Lamsden: 112; Lords Gallery: 53;   Lowry Estate: 142–3; M.C.C.: 16 (top and bottom), 22,
32 (right), 49, 56, 78 (right and left), 80 (right), 84 (top), 85 (top), 92, 101 (bottom), 105, 137, 144 (bottom),
149 (top);   Phillips: 17, 104;   Retrograph Archive: 76 (top), 85 (bottom), 97 (bottom), 109;   Ralph Steadman/
Abner Stein: 140; Surrey County Cricket Club: 21.

# Contents

# Preface

Some explanation is needed to define more exactly the title that embraces the cover. This 'history' does not set out to be conterminal with those already on the shelves. The scholarly tomes of Altham and Swanton, the lucid narrative of Parker and the idiosyncratic and sometimes deliberately perverse offering of Bowen, together with others of a more restricted nature, are valued by all who seek to learn of cricket's past. Our study of an often disconnected train of events lingers in relatively modest precincts. In fact, to call it a history of cricket per se, is somewhat imprecise. The emphasis lies as a survey of the game throughout its correlation with the English people and those who have had a connection with their way of life.

Naturally, within a prescribed number of words and a set amount of illustration, broad brush strokes and skeletal lines have to be drawn rather than a discursive, comprehensive approach adopted. That is not to preclude an occasional foray into less-trodden areas or a bypassing of more popular resorts. Indeed, taking as read a fundamental object of any book, which is to entertain and perhaps inform, emphasis has purposely been placed where documentation and representation are not so obvious. The ancestry of anything, especially cricket, has bare essentials that it is mandatory to record, yet to recapitulate *all* that has been stated and shown before would be a futile exercise.

One fascination of cricket is that it never ceases to fascinate. To become a devotee in childhood means being hooked for life. Happily it is an addiction for which there is no need of legislation nor government health warnings.

Cricket at Wittersham in Kent attributed
to Charles Deane.

# 1

# Plebeians and Patricians

Cricket being played by village boys in
close proximity to the church. The
original is a pen and ink and brown wash,
signed with monogram and dated 1783.

When and where did cricket begin? No one knows nor ever will. Historians, trying to beat a path through convoluted cul-de-sacs back to an immaculate conception, have usually lost their way in impenetrable semantic jungles.

Many imaginative leaps back to the Dark Ages and beyond have decided that in one way or another the game evolved from, for example, stob-ball, handyn and handoute, cat and dog and even a Persian pastime called chugar or chugan. French *criquet*, Anglo-Saxon *crec*, Danish *krykke* and German *krücke* are proposed as generic terms, and the ball games of Ancient Egypt and Lydia as embryonic forms. Enthusiastic explorers like Percy Thomas – H.P.-T., H.J. Massingham and recently the learned Heiner Gillmeister, have spent incalculable hours on etymological studies, a fraction of which would cause a time-and-motion expert to blanch before trying to cost the components of a fantastical Tardis.

All of it, in a way, has led nowhere – which is not to disparage much valuable research. Possibilities have been limited and probabilities listed. We can speculate that the game's gynaecological wards were in the Kentish Weald, on the Hampshire Down or on a Flanders and Normandy field. We can presume that shepherds, not watching their flocks by day but disporting themselves by clobbering stones with their crooks, were the first cricketers. We do not know for certain.

Naturally recourse has been made to ancient scribes. Claims for enlightenment from the writings of visionaries like Eustathius, Archbishop of Thessalonia, *c*. 750, and Josephus Iscanus, a twelfth-century cleric of Exeter, who wrote:

> *The youth at cricks did play,*
> *Throughout the livelong day,*

have been lightly lanced. So too, one suspects, has the idea that the Vespasian version of the 23rd Psalm hints of a bat in a sporting context.

Illuminated manuscripts have also been scrutinized, generating flickers of light for those inclined to associate unformed figures holding clubs and globules with whichever game they fancy. Deserved attention has been given to Bede's Life of St. Cuthbert, *c*. 1120–30; a decretal issued by Pope Gregory IX, *c*. 1230; the Schilling M.S., *c*. 1300; and The Romance of Alexander, *c*. 1340, as well

Illuminated manuscript at the Bodleian Library from Bede's *Life of St. Cuthbert*, who when young 'played atte balle' with children. Dated *c*. 1120–30.

(*Right*) The Boy with a Bat, namely, Walter Hawkesworth Fawkes, who started life as Walter Ramsden Beaumont. Robin Simon and Alastair Smart have commented in *Art of Cricket* that the painting 'is of especial interest in that it shows the two stumps of the period (*c*. 1760) not as forked twigs but as flat pieces of wood with notches carved in their tops'. Newark Castle is in the background. The painting is ascribed to the prolific Thomas Hudson.

A 7 × 4 in. hand-painted magic lantern slide set in wood. The lever action controls the movement of ball and bat.

as others of their kind. The last is a case in point, for Robert Henderson, in his book *Ball, Bat and Bishop*, associates the drawing with the French game *la soule*. A fourteenth-century ivory carving from Paris, held in the Schnütgen Museum at Cologne, has also excited interest, though it is difficult to escape the conclusion that none of these basically embryonic artistic endeavours relay more than a shared root for most recreations with club-and-missile.

It was, however, the publication, by the Society of Antiquaries in 1787, of the wardrobe accounts of King Edward I for the year 1300, that really gave pause for thought. One entry shows reimbursement to the chaplain, John de Leck, for equipment and clothing used by his son, the Prince, at creag, generally accepted as an antecedent of cricket.

Some thirty years later, in 1330, William Pagula, vicar of Winkfield, near Windsor, wrote a Latin poem advising parish priests to forbid the playing of ball games in churchyards:

> *Bat and bares and suche play*
> *Out of chyrche-yarde put away*

Among other sports, Pagula could have been referring to stoolball rather than creag or cricketts, but the lines are at least a timely reminder of the relationship between church and the noble game throughout its recognized existence.

But for the medieval clerical and judicial establishments' opposition to ball games in churchyards, we would know even less of cricket's pre-history, as it may be termed, than we do. Many unfortunate country folk suffered the consequences of putting bat to ball in the wrong place. In 1622, at Boxgrove in Sussex, nine parishioners were prosecuted for playing in God's acre on a Sunday and seven years later there was a similar event at Ruckinge, near Romney Marsh, in Kent.

This time, paradoxically, a hound was caught running with the hares. The local curate, an ex-King's College, Cambridge, man called Henry Cuffin, was up before the beak in the Archdeacon's Court for having spent several Sunday afternoons playing 'at cricketts, in very unseemly manner with boys, and other very mean and base persons to the great scandal of his ministerie'. Disgraceful! How could he? The poor curate tried his hardest to raise some seem by pointing out that at least, like his egg, he was partly good because his parishioners were not mean or base but 'persons of repute and fashion' – all to no avail.

There were a few such incidents, though the parson was not always present or nabbed. Cricket, which is likely to have started as a pastime for children,

Part of the relevant section in the Guildford Court Book that includes the world *creckett* (cricket) – the earliest known surviving example.

A game at Dupper Fields, Marylebone. 1793 is the given date but notice the use of two stumps.

*Miss Wicket and Miss Trigger.* A cricket print from the original picture of John Collet sold by Carington Bowles at his map and print warehouse in St. Paul's Churchyard, London, 1778.

*Mifs Trigger you fee is an excellent Shot*
*And forty-five Notches Mifs Wickets juft got.*

had by now, in the seventeenth century, become an established means for the plebs to get rid of their pew-ache. What better way for the lower orders to ease cramped limbs after a long church service than to disport themselves at cricket and other pursuits in the yard outside? Sunday was their one free day and the enclosure's surface was relatively smooth compared to some of the rough fields nearby. At that time, also, churchyards were less encumbered with gravestones. It is no wonder that in several cathedrals and churches there are still murals and stained glass depicting figures brandishing crics (crooks) and spherical objects.

For the would-be seeker of source material, however, there is precious little to convey the true nature of cricket, though that little is truly precious. Most students acknowledge 'Stonyhurst Cricket', a single-wicket game with an oddly-shaped club just over three feet long and a stone wicket, as a variation on a theme. It was probably played consecutively at Eu in Normandy, St. Omer, Bruges and then Liège for over two hundred years from the late sixteenth century, following the travels of the English College before settling at Stonyhurst Hall near Preston in Lancashire. So between 1598, when at a Land Tribunal in Guildford John Derrick testified to playing cricket as a schoolboy during the 1550s, and the year 1700, when the thrice-weekly *Post Boy* advertised in effect a mini-Test series on Clapham Common with £600 prize money at stake, there are some fifty to sixty known recorded references to the game. As the reign of William of Orange progressed, then gave way to those of Anne and George I, the reduction of state control over the press, the broadening tastes of the public and, above all, the increasing countenance of cricket, persuaded newspaper editors to include the occasional line or two to whet coffee-house gossip.

The game was gradually becoming more or less accepted by those in power, though still consigned to the level of amusements for 'citizens and peasants' alongside bear-baiting and throwing at cocks. Its transition from a solely working-class activity had been advanced by the intervention of politics. Around the period of the Civil War and after, many Royalists thought it prudent to spend a great deal of time on their country estates, away from London and its potentially hostile environs. These landed gentry had much time to while away and may have thought that by taking part in a previously plebeian pastime they were doing no harm whatsoever to their prospects in the longevity stakes.

Other stakes soon became very much a part of this fascinating diversion. Not the sort that Cromwell's commissioners had in mind when in 1656 they proscribed 'krickett' throughout Ireland and the common hangman burned every stick and ball to be found, notwithstanding the legend that 'Old Ironsides' himself supposedly liked the occasional knock. Rather the nobility's addiction to betting, which, if not proving Gogol's claims that 'gambling is the great leveller', certainly brought about a reliance by the gentry on the skills of those they would regard as their social inferiors.

By the time the eighteenth century got under way, and social mores allowed overt aristocratic involvement, huge sums were being wagered on the outcome of matches. *The Sporting Kalendar* reported three encounters between All-England and Eton at Newmarket in 1751 at which the stakes were £1,500 with almost £20,000 at risk in side bets. Five hundred or a thousand guineas on offer, winners taking all, was not uncommon in Georgian times.

The first full description of a cricket match came in a collection of Latin verse, '*Musae Juveniles*', published in 1706: *In Certamen Pilae* was resurrected in 1922, having mouldered for over two hundred years in a 'literary lumber-room'. The author, William Goldwin, an old Etonian and graduate of King's College, Cambridge, performed a signal service for posterity by throwing considerable light on the evolution of the game and its laws.

The earliest written rules governing the playing of cricket, though, are likely to have disappeared for ever. The first code extant, the Articles of Agreement drawn up in 1727 between the second Duke of Richmond and Gordon and Mr. Alan Brodrick, of Pepperharowe, Surrey, for two 12-a-side matches concentrate mostly on procedures and conduct, not method. One concludes that there was no doubt about collective compliance with basic regulations, and these agreements were merely supplementary to a known code.

Important cricket matches, with or without proforma, came about through the entrepreneurial instincts of wealthy landowners. A pioneer who led the way in the 1720s was one Edwin Stede, 'the Father of Kent cricket', whose ancestral Hall occupied high ground near Harrietsham. Stede gambled heavily on cards and tried to recoup his losses at cricket, though in 1724, when his team was

involved in a lawsuit against Chingford, there was no quick return for outlay. The Essex side, with defeat in sight, had refused to continue the match, and Lord Chief Justice Pratt, who would seem to have had little interest in matters sporting, carefully ducked the issue by ordering the game to be finished off on Dartford Heath, a sort of halfway house. It took two years to get the match re-started. The legal establishment was obviously divided in 1726, for in Kent the warring sides were falling in line by executing the ruling of the then late Lord Chief Justice, while in neighbouring Essex, at Writtle, a Justice of the Peace was dispersing innocent cricketers, convinced that the game was a pretext to gather disaffected crowds for potential rebellion.

We have already noted the interest in cricket of the Duke of Richmond, grandson of Charles II and Louise de Quérouaille, Duchess of Portsmouth. He was a generous patron who employed a handful of cricketers to work on his estate at Goodwood. In August of 1731, he set out for Richmond Green, in Surrey, to lead a team against one headed by a local gent, Mr. Chambers, for £100 a side. Having been delayed on the journey the Duke arrived late, resulting in the opposition being left with too little time in which to force a victory. The mob, inflamed with drink and suspecting a fix, rioted, verbally and physically attacking his Grace and his team, some of whom had their shirts torn from their backs. Possibly as a result of this unruly behaviour, the Duke became less absorbed in cricketing matters thereafter, leaving the game in Sussex to be organized by Sir William Gage of Firle, Member of Parliament for Seaford.

An employee on the Duke's country seat who turned out regularly for Gage's sides was Thomas Waymark, 'the father of cricket professionals'. Waymark was thought to be a groom and he personifies the practice of those with proven skill at cricket being engaged in other capacities between games. The custom even extended to 'lending out' players to friendly rivals when fixtures did not clash. Thus did noblemen bolster their chances in matches with much at stake.

Eventually Waymark moved to Berkshire and played cricket for a Bray miller named Darville. It is cruelly ironic that a player so celebrated for his 'agility and dexterity' in the field is remembered chiefly for dropping a decisive catch. In the grand match between Kent and England at the Artillery Ground in 1744 Kent's last pair were together, needing three runs to win, when Waymark spilled a skier. The subsequent victory left the unfortunate fielder taking the blame and being dubbed, in another era, by Andrew Lang, 'immortal butterfingers'.

William Hodsoll (known as Hodswell), owner of a tannery in Dartford, was one of that last pair for Kent. He was said to be the fastest underarm bowler of his time and, judging from James Love's poem of the match, the England batsmen must have felt they were being subjected to a virtual cannonade, as the ball . . .

> . . . whizz'd along, with unimagin'd force,
> and bore down all, resistless in its course.

*Cricket: an Heroic Poem* was penned by Love or Dance, to give him his real name, at the tender literary age of 22. He was the son of George Dance, architect and designer of the Mansion House in London and educated at Merchant Taylors' and St. John's, Oxford. Dance, perhaps unsure of his vocation, soon went bankrupt before finding his feet on the theatrical boards as an actor, director and manager. The verses, in three books, are an important landmark in the recording of cricket because for the first time there is an indication of the run of play and the form of the participants. Among the players in the England

The portrait by Almond of Edward 'Lumpy' Stevens, the most relentlessly accurate of early underhand bowlers.

(*Right*) The earliest bat yet found. James (sometimes referred to as John) Chitty of Knaphill, Surrey, made sure of his ownership. The bat is kept at the Oval.

(*Previous page*) Cricket played by the Gentlemen's Club, White Conduit House, a long boundary throw from the Pentonville Road, London, in 1784. Robert Dighton, portrait painter and caricaturist, included this drawing as one of a series of six British Sports.

side were Richard Newland, of Slindon in Sussex, the leading left-handed bats-man of his time, and his brothers, Adam and John. It was to be 136 years before such fraternity was equalled by the brothers Grace. Newland made the highest score in both innings from either side.

Scoring well for Kent in that famous victory was Valentine Romney, acknow-ledged 'by universal consent the greatest cricketer in the world'. Journalists of the day never lacked superlatives when shaping their encomiums. Romney was another whose prowess enabled him to enjoy a certain security in the employ of the aristocracy: he worked as a gardener on the Sackville estate. It is salutory to compare Romney's lot with that of a modern cricketing 'super-star' who perhaps would not even consider pruning his own prize blooms.

Opening the batting for the hop county was the extraordinary 'Long Robin', whose pseudonym disguised less wholesome activities. When not scoring freely for Kent or promoting matches at the Artillery Ground Robert Colchin, for that was his real name, frequented the twilight world of London riff-raff, 'disgra-cing himself with every impolite accomplishment'. In the *Connoisseur* of 1756 his vulgarities, attributed to one 'Toby Bumper' to avoid litigation, were reck-oned to include 'drinking purl in the morning, eating black puddings at Bar-tholomew Fair, boxing with Buckhorse; and also that he was frequently engaged at the Artillery Ground with Faulkner and Dungate at cricket'. Apparently Col-chin found great amusement in aping the manners and speech of the coarser elements of society and was often to be seen with street-walkers in such murky areas of the city as Helmet Court and Vinegar Yard, off Charing Cross and Covent Garden, and in the shadowy dives and back alleys that were the abode of thieves. His persona – a member of the gentility with considerable means – was a carefully contrived front to mask his life as a gang leader in the London underworld. The capital was riddled with crime and the playwright, Henry Fielding, was soon to formulate his plan for a new police force, the Bow Street Runners. Colchin, in effect, was a predecessor of the Krays of our time, affecting a demeanour to hide misdemeanour and manipulating others to do his dirty work. He, like them, enjoyed boxing, was an habitué of the prize-ring, was known to have dusted knuckles with the 'grandaddy of self-defence', the legend-ary waterman, Jack Broughton and, as we have seen, swopped uppercuts also with the slippery booth pugilist Buckhorse (preferred to John Smith), who would allow himself to be knocked down by anyone for a trifling gratuity.

It is easy to forget that the veneer of civilized behaviour was easily punctured, or in fact non-existent, in the eighteenth century. For the majority life was a desperate struggle to avoid the poorhouse. Escape was sought in various ways and many avenues led to the river. Other flights from reality were less solitary or final. The consumption of liquor and pursuit of pleasure gave temporary relief, quickly dispelled when disillusionment followed, often the result of rash betting undertaken in moments of euphoria. With livelihoods at risk, fear fuelled anger when sporting events did not go according to plan. Naturally cricket was not immune, the players just as susceptible.

At a game between Brompton and London on Chelsea Common in 1731 a dispute led to the two sides fighting for half an hour 'and most of the Brompton gentlemen were forced to fly for quarters and some retired home with black eyes and broken heads, much to the satisfaction of the opposite side'. Then at Chatham in 1758 local cricketers threatened to murder the Superintendant of the Lines unless he permitted them to play on land they regarded as theirs. At Tilbury in 1776, for a match between Kent and Essex, an objection was raised to one of the players, sparking off a battle with guns and bayonets commandeered from the local Fort that resulted in several deaths. Eleven years later, at Hinckley, it was the turn of the crowd. In soccer-hooligan fashion, at the end of a game between Leicester and Coventry, supporters ran amok through the town.

The need for money was not always apparent. In 1787 a butcher of Pluckley (let us avoid the obvious limerick) called Thomas Ballard committed suicide in his slaughterhouse after 'being at cricket the same evening'. Who knows why? On a far happier financial note, the London Magazine reported that in 1739 a Croydon farmer for a wager bowled a cricket ball all the way to London Bridge. It took 455 deliveries.

Throughout the 1700s the antics of cricketers and the idiosyncrasies of the game itself were mirrored in all manner of literary effusions, magazines, plays, books of sermons, broadsheets and verse. One epistle favoured the concealment of anonymity to take a scurrilous swipe at those bosom buddies and great cricket-

A rectangular nineteenth-century papier-mâché snuff-box with a painted lid on which there is a certain conflation of eighteenth and nineteenth-century details.

A page from the old Hambledon Minute Book outlining the standing toasts.

The LAWS of the NOBLE GAME of CRICKET,
as Established at the Star and Garter Pall-Mall by a Committee of Noblemen and Gentlemen

A linen commemorative handkerchief, printed in purple, showing cricket at the White Conduit Club with the laws of the game accessible to those with keen eyesight and a magnifying glass. Half-length portraits of the Prince of Wales, Sir Horatio Mann, Colonel Tarleton and the Duke of Dorset. An edge embroidered '*W.C.W.*' *circa*, 1785.

lovers, the misanthropic Earl of Tankerville and the gregarious Duke of Dorset. It was addressed to 'two of the idlest Lords in his Majesty's three Kingdoms':

> *When Death (for Lords must die) your doom shall seal,*
> *What sculptur'd Honours shall your tomb reveal?*
> *Instead of Glory, with a weeping eye,*
> *Instead of Virtue pointing to the sky,*
> *Let Bat and Ball th'affronted stone disgrace,*
> *While Farce stands leering by, with Satyr face,*
> *Holding, with forty notches mark'd a board –*
> *The* noble *triumph of a* noble *Lord!*

The Duke had just scored forty runs in a recent match and the affronted poet obviously felt that to dally at the wicket when the country was on a war footing was highly irresponsible. No doubt the rhymster – none other than the Earl of Derby – was also affronted by the fact that his wife, the Countess, was having an affair with Dorset. In the event the Duke was sent as Ambassador to Paris in 1782 and was involved in the aborted '89 tour, of which more later.

Dorset was not alone of his kind in being addicted to cricket. Its more eminent devotees included the Earl of Sandwich, to whom Love's poem had been dedicated; Sir Horatio Mann, with estates at Bishopsbourne and Linton Park, who preferred cricket on horseback with long bats and said he played better on four legs than most men on two; the Earl of Winchilsea and the Hon. Charles Lennox, who were closely involved in the founding of the MCC; Lord Strathavon of Aldermaston; Lord Chesterfield and Sir Peter Burrell.

The Duke's fellow recipient of such scathing censure, Charles Bennett, Earl of Tankerville and sometime Postmaster-General, had a country seat at Mount Felix, near Walton-on-Thames, and he, not unexpectedly, patronized Surrey cricket. In his service acting as a butler was the stylish batsman William Bedster – he eventually transferred his allegiance to Middlesex – while out-of-doors, working as a gardener, was the celebrated Edward 'Lumpy' Stevens.

'Lumpy' was a deadly-accurate slow-medium bowler whose services were much in demand by the aristocratic fraternity. His ability was severely tested one day when he managed, during a four-delivery over, to pitch a ball on to a feather that had been placed on the ground. His grateful employer pocketed a £100 bet.

When the revised laws of 1774 gave the choice of pitch to visiting bowlers, 'Lumpy' invariably chose the downward slope, which assisted his shooters. He 'castled' the great John Small of Hambledon on one memorable occasion and morally defeated him three times more in the second innings, the ball whistling between the two-stump wicket but leaving it intact. As an indirect consequence of this and similar occurrences, some years later the third stump was added.

The genial 'Lumpy' was supposed to have acquired his sobriquet from a rotundity nurtured by an exceptional appetite. At a Hambledon dinner he was witnessed consuming a large apple-pie that had been baked for the whole team. This unedifying spectacle left the assembled company bereft not only of a dessert but also of speech.

A less lumpy 'Lumpy' was reputed to have been 'a bit of a smuggler' when young – no doubt purloining comestibles – and somewhere there is a depiction of him dancing with a jug of ale in his hand. The well-known portrait at Knole House was discovered by one of cricket's leading historians, John Goulstone.

The story of Hambledon is, of course, a indelible part of the cricket tapestry

and has been told many times. Invariably retelling good stories can make them better, but no amount of exaggeration can diminish the achievements and importance of Hambledon as a vital staging-post on cricket's long journey from children's pastime to modern-day maturity. It is essential, however, to retain a clear perspective. If there had been a Nyren to rejoice over the deeds of, for instance, Dartford, Slindon, Mitcham and Farnham, there always would have been a more balanced view in surveys of early cricket. At different periods, all these villages produced sides to match metropolitan or All-England combinations. How we miss eulogies on William Bedle, 'formerly the most expert player in England', or Thomas Pattenden or William Bowra!

It should be borne in mind, too, that the labelling of teams could be a matter of convenience; a generic term when that applied or the name of the patron and promoter even when the side was inherently that of somewhere else. Hampshire called itself Hambledon on occasions when players were included from outside the county boundary, and there are endless examples of counties and clubs finding places for talented 'foreigners'.

Most would agree that the Hambledon Club owed its foundation to a few old boys of Westminster School, principally the Rev. Charles Powlett (sometimes Paulet), vicar of Itchen Abbas, who was the son of the third Duke of Bolton by Lavinia Felton (Mrs. Bestwick), the Polly Peachum of Gay's *Beggar's Opera*. Fellow backers and prominent members were The Hon. Charles Lennox, grandson of the second Duke of Richmond, of the 1727 Articles fame, the Earl of Winchilsea, Philip Dehaney, Henry Bonham and the quixotically-christened Jervoise Clark Jervoise.

The 'General' of Hambledon was Richard Nyren, secretary, captain, landlord of the *Bat and Ball* inn and father of John, chronicler of their doings. His team of yeomen players represented a range of country trades, being bakers, cobblers, potters, carpenters, farmers and gamekeepers. Their names are now etched in the annals of cricket: David Harris, John Small, Tom Sueter, George Leer, Noah Mann, Thomas Brett, the Walkers, Barber, Hogsflesh and Buck. Buck, a nickname for Peter Stewart, was the self-appointed wag of the side. When Hambledon played away from home the complete eleven plus umpire and scorer travelled in a large caravan drawn by a pair of sturdy horses. Nyren records that on one occasion 'the vehicle having been overturned, and the whole cargo unshipped, Buck remained at his post, and refused to come out, desiring that they would right the vessel with him in it, as "one good turn deserved another".'

The financial rewards for players were not great. For a three or four-day match they might expect between seven and nine shillings each, which, compared with an estimated 'take' of over £22,000 from fifty-one matches against England in ten years alone, marks an almost criminal discrepancy between patricians and plebeians.

The club's colours were sky-blue, and members wore coats of that colour with black velvet collars and the letters CC engraved on their buttons, at different times donning velvet caps or silver-laced hats.

For 'class' matches of the time the standard dress was similar: frilled shirts, nankeen breeches, silk stockings and leather shoes with buckles that could cause a nasty injury to an unwary fielder. One is reminded of 'Silver Billy' Beldham's story of John Wells tearing off a finger-nail by trapping his finger in his shoe-buckle on picking up a ball.

Headgear was usually of the three-cornered or jockey type, decorated with the colour lace of the team. The Caterham Club in Surrey, one of the most

*Quite Cricket*, by Graham Clarke, 1983, $13\frac{1}{2} \times 21\frac{1}{4}$ in. Graham Clarke's hand-coloured etchings portray a vision of England locked in a timeless pastoral idyll – in a sense, medievalism brought up-to-date. A recent description of his approach noted that 'Disregarding formal perspective, he crams his patchwork countryside with twisty lanes, windmills, haystacks, snug pubs, cottages and ancient churches, often lit by a curiously combined sun and moon which he calls a "heavenly orb"'. Naturally, such Englishness encompasses cricket.

powerful combinations in the country during the patronage of Henry Rowed in the 1760s, wore silver-laced hats with the single exception of Rowed himself. This local farmer of considerable means obviously wanted to be distinguishable from the common herd and so he favoured a gold-laced hat. He became known as 'the Golden Farmer of Katerham'.

The craftsmen producing cricketing artefacts seemed to prefer the air across the county border in Kent. Rhodes made bats at Maidstone, Petts did the same at Sevenoaks, Clout's constructed balls in the same town and Duke and Son diversified from leather boots to leather cricket balls at Penshurst. The wooden sphere had long since vanished and the presentation to the thirteen year-old Prince of Wales in 1775 of the first treble-sewn cricket ball marked a growing sophistication in the trade. But the Kentish bat and ball makers did not have the field entirely to themselves; George Wheeler was issuing his trade cards at Brick Lane, Whitechapel, and later on Aquila Clapshaw opened a workshop at Turnham Green.

Down in Hampshire old John Small made bats and balls for much of his eighty-nine years and taught his son to do the same. The premises at Petersfield exhibited a pride not easily dismissed:

*'Here lives John Small*
*Sells bats and balls*
*And will play any man in England'*

The early bats were curved, with long handles, and had had no specified dimensions until 1771, when during a match between Chertsey and Hambledon 'Shock' White arrived at the crease with an implement as wide as the wicket. Shortly afterwards the maximum width was fixed at $4\frac{1}{4}$ inches.

'Long Bob' Robinson (not to be confused with 'Long Robin'), so-called because of his length and weight, was another, like White, who had to submit to the indignity of having his bat shaved down to size with a penknife. The accomplished left-hander for Surrey was not best pleased: 'I'll pay you out for spoiling my bat!' and with the adrenalin running furiously he played one of his best innings. Robinson, also known as 'Three-fingered Jack', had a bat specially grooved and strengthened with iron to accommodate his disability. He is credited with inventing leg-guards when he wore thin board splints to protect his shins. The impact of the ball produced a clatter that caused a great deal of hilarity, so much so that he eventually gave up the idea. Another of Robinson's innovations was to try spikes 'of monstrous length' but only on one shoe. Eventually he moved to Holt, in Norfolk, and helped to produce a great cricketer for another generation by coaching the young Fuller Pilch.

Cricket too was moving on. As the end of the eighteenth century came in sight the game became more centralized. The focus changed to Lord's while Hambledon, Slindon and Kent receded into glorious memory. The Marylebone Club started to become the official voice of cricket, its jurisdiction known country-wide. Laws were constituted, modified and published in the annual *Complete List of all the Grand Matches* by the official scorer to the MCC, Samuel Britcher. The character of cricket began to change and so did the cast. The game was growing up. A new era had begun.

(*Left*) Posed figure portraits extracted from a single page in the notebook of George Shepheard, Snr., who played for Surrey. The watercolour sketches are of the leading cricketing personalities of the day, *c.* 1790.

Copper engraving by Cook. Published on July 1st, 1793 by I. Wheble, Warwick Square, London. Frontispiece to the June issue, 1793 of *The Sporting Magazine*. The magazine also printed the laws of cricket and there were deficiencies in omission of lbw and the third stump. The picture shows the out-of-date two stump game.

Cricket on College Field, Eton, *c*. 1843.
William Evans the painter was born,
educated and became drawing master at
Eton.

# 2

# Slowly Maturing

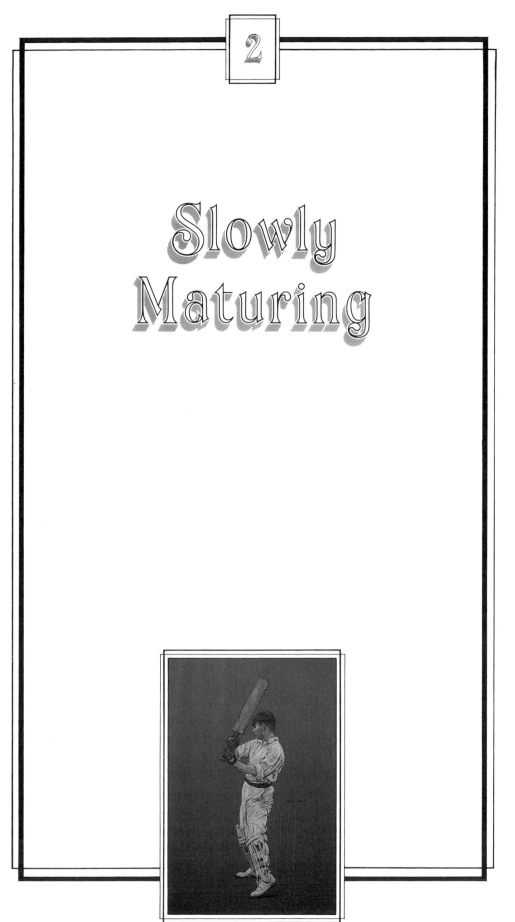

# A GRAND CRICKET MATCH, Play'd between Eleven Men of all ENGLAND, againſt Thirty-three of the County of NORFÓLK,

## On SWAFHAM RACE GROUND, Monday July 17th, 1797. and two following Days.

### For FIVE HUNDRED GUINEAS.

c ſtands for *caicht out.* b. ſtands for *bowl'd out,* and s. for *ſtump'd out,*

| NORFOLK, | No. of Notches. First Innings. | | No. of Notches. Second Innings. | |
|---|---|---|---|---|
| Mr. Brown, | 6 | b, T. Walker, | 0 | s, Hammond, |
| Sculfer, | 1 | run out, | 2 | c, H. Walker, |
| M. Raven, | 3 | c, Fennex, | 1 | c, ditto, |
| Harmer, | 0 | c, Hammond, | 9 | b, Lord Beauclerk, |
| James Fuller, | 7 | c, Lord Beauclerk, | 0 | b, ditto, |
| Jackſon, | 1 | c, Freemantle, | 0 | b, ditto, |
| Stibbard. | 0 | s, Hammond, | 9 | b, Fennex, |
| Rev'd. Mr. Allen, | 5 | b, Wells, | 2 | b, ditto, |
| John Fuller, | 6 | c, Beldam, | 1 | ran out, |
| Archer, | 9 | b, Wells, | 9 | b, Wells, |
| R. Raven, | 0 | c, H. Walker, | 2 | b, Lord Beauclerk, |
| Cock, | 1 | b, Lord Beauclerk, | 7 | c, ditto, |
| James Withers, | 0 | c, Hammond, | 0 | b, Wells, |
| Brooks, | 0 | b, Wells, | 0 | s, Hammond, |
| Ruſt, | 1 | c, Beldam, | 3 | b, Wells, |
| G. Withers. | 0 | c, ditto, | 4 | s, Hammond, |
| Bayfield Fuller, | 0 | c, Hammond, | 0 | c. Wells, |
| Rayner, | 0 | b, Lord Beauclerk, | 0 | c, H. Walker, |
| Curtis, | 0 | c, Small, | 8 | c, Fennex, |
| Rumbal, | 0 | c, Fennex, | 0 | b, ditto, |
| Bennet, | 0 | c, Hammond, | 3 | s, Hammond, |
| Ulph, | 0 | b, Lord Beauclerk, | 0 | c, ditto, |
| Sturley, | 1 | b. Wells, | 0 | b, Fennex, |
| Paul, | 2 | s, Hammond, | 0 | b, Lord Beauclerk, |
| Scott, | 0 | c, Lord Beauclerk, | 0 | c, H. Walker, |
| Watlin, | 0 | c, Beldam, | 1 | leg before wicket, |
| Milligan, | 6 | b, Lord Beauclerk, | 0 | b, Wells, |
| Mitchel, | 0 | b, Lord Beauclerk, | 14 | leg before wicket, |
| Ben. Fuller, | 1 | c, H. Walker, | 0 | b, Wells, |
| Laſcock, | 0 | not out | 0 | c, Small, |
| Cuſhing, | 0 | run out | 0 | c, Wells, |
| Emerſon, | 0 | b, Lord Beauclerk, | 0 | c, Fennex, |
| Warner, | 0 | b, ditto, | 1 | not out. |
| Bye runs | 0 | | 5 | |
| | 50 | | 81 | Total 131 |

| ALL ENGLAND. | | | | |
|---|---|---|---|---|
| Mr. T. Walker, | 55 | c, Scott, | | |
| Fennex, | 4 | b, Millgan, | | |
| Small, | 2 | c, Sculfer, | | |
| Freemantle, | 4 | b, G. Withers, | | |
| Robinſon, | 2 | c, Rayner, | | |
| Lord Beauclerk, | 39 | c, Emerſon, | | |
| Hon. T. Tufton, | 19 | c, Archer, | | |
| Hammond, | 10 | c, J. Fuller, | | |
| Beldam, | 6 | not out, | | |
| H. Walker, | 0 | b, Ben. Fuller, | | |
| Wells, | 3 | c, Warner | | |
| Bye runs | 0 | | | |
| | 144 | | | |

All England won at One Innings, by 13 runs.

Cricket had reached a natural watershed. The Artillery Ground at Islington had had its day and now so too had White Conduit Fields. For the upper-crust cronies of the *Star and Garter*, lessee Robert Bartholomew's meadow, close by Pentonville, had become far too populated by those for whom it was designed. They preferred to display their form in more select company, so the attendant to their cricketing needs, Thomas Lord, was dispatched with urgency to find a new patch on which they could scatter their strokes and their fortunes.

The new ground, on the Portman estate, lay at the edge of the built-up area by the New Road, leading to Paddington. At that time London was twelve times the size of any other conurbation in the kingdom, stretching four miles from east to west and two miles from north to south. It housed nearly a million souls, an eighth of the population, the majority living in great poverty and a minority with great riches. Much of what we now think of as the capital was in the county of Middlesex; there were cricket clubs in nearly every district.

Lord's ground attracted the paying customer straight away. Over two thousand attended a match in its first year, 1787, and the refreshment tents and accommodation received unanimous approval; 'the utility of the batten-fence was made very evident, as it kept out all improper spectators', noted the local press.

Two noblemen adopting high profiles in setting up the new club were the Earl of Winchilsea, whose urbanity never wavered, even when he suffered heavy losses through bets on cricket, and the mercurial Charles Lennox, who was to become the fourth Duke of Richmond in 1806. Lennox had a most spectacular and eventful career, to which it is impossible to do justice except in random impressionistic form. At various times he fought a duel with the Duke of York (of nursery rhyme immortality) and another with a pamphleteer called Theophilus Swift, who had maligned his character; the unfortunate Swift was unable to live up to his surname and was injured, though not fatally. Having gained practice, Lennox then took part in a larger conflict, at Waterloo with Wellington, and between times helped produce fourteen children in a fertile marriage. He also sought job-satisfaction as commander of a battalion of the Coldstream Guards, as Governor-General of British North America, as Lord Lieutenant of Ireland and as Prime Minister of Great Britain. The last office was the only one to elude him. None of these minor callings or inconveniences

(*Far left*) A famous match with legendary figures playing for *All England*.

A bat housed in the Lords' Museum made by Charles Clapshaw, b. 1776 d. 1851.

(*Right*) The bevelled-back pine 2½ lb. bat that was 'Silver Billy' Beldham's. Infested by woodworm, creosoted as was the custom in pre-Rentokil days and charred at the bottom from years of hanging over an open fireplace, as described so graphically by the Rev. James Pycroft. For bringing this priceless artefact of the legendary Farnham and England cricketer back into public view, cricket-lovers owe everything to the editor of the Surrey Advertiser, Graham Collyer. A chance conversation with a relative of the Cleave family (descended from the bat-makers of that name who merged with Charles Clapshaw's, the makers of Beldham's bat), led to a visit to Malvern where Collyer made his 'find' in a glass case above a window-seat.

Beldham, who retired from front rank cricket in the early 1820s, was landlord of the Barley Mow at Tilford. He fathered nine children from two wives, not 39 as has often been stated. He died aged 96 in 1862 and is buried in Tilford churchyard.

An early nineteenth-century illustration for a child's book of games.

Cricket.

London, Published by Tabart & Co July 13 1804.

(*Below*) A Staffordshire figurine that some maintain depicts George Parr and Julius Caesar, but who can be sure.

Grand Cricket Match at Lord's, 1837.
John Moore.

prevented Lennox playing cricket, which he did with panache wherever he happened to be. In retrospect one has the impression that he happened to be in
a great many different places at odd moments – usually when a dispute was
occupying the bodies, if not the minds, of those in the vicinity, so it is quite
unsurprising to find this most engaging individualist playing cricket on the
Heights of Abraham at a significant moment of history.

His death was equally bizarre. In 1819, when visiting a military post at Sorel,
on the south bank of the St. Lawrence River in Canada, he was bitten on the
hand by a tame fox. Undeterred, he continued his tour of duty and stopped
off at a new settlement named, in his honour, Richmondville. At dinner that
evening the Duke remarked to a fellow officer: 'I don't know how it is, Cockburn,
but I cannot relish my wine tonight as usual, and I feel that if I were a dog
I should be shot for a mad one!' Within hours that prescient thought was close
to consummation. The feverish nobleman was reluctantly persuaded on to a
boat for conveyance down river in search of medical help, but after a short
distance the sight and sound of water became unbearable to him. He seized
the boatman by the throat and forced him to row for the shore, then leaped
from the vessel and ran like the possessed man he was until caught and taken
to shelter in a nearby farmhouse. The stricken Duke died in agony shortly afterwards from hydrophobia.

Meanwhile many somewhat less dramatic events had been happening in home
arenas. Thomas Lord had helped establish the ground bearing his name as the
new centre of the cricketing universe, a cachet that attracted big matches and
big money. In 1791 there was a game between twenty-two of Middlesex and
the Hambledon Club for a thousand guineas. Even though they out-numbered

(*Next page*) *The Cricketers*, Peter de Wint (1784–1849). Watercolour by the Staffordshire-born son of a Dutch-American.

their opponents by two to one, Middlesex only just managed to secure victory by scoring 96 for 18 in the last innings. In that year also the county won two encounters with the Marylebone Club, though Marylebone members had engaged the services of two highly regarded professionals, Purchase and Beldham. 'Silver Billy' Beldham was much in demand, says Nyren, during the last decade of the 1700s; he 'rapidly attained to the extraordinary accomplishment of being the finest player that has appeared within the latitude of more than half a century'.

If Beldham was rated so highly he did not lack competition. Lord Frederick Beauclerk was beginning to slip into gear and there were worthy exponents of other cricketing crafts – Thomas Boxall, an exacting bowler, and John Hammond, an adept wicket-keeper. A dip into Britcher's annual scorecards reveals a school of hardy practitioners and principals who were ever present at notable matches: the honourable Tuftons, Colonel Bligh, Captain Cumberland, Lord Darnley, William Fennex, G. Leycester, esquire, and scraggy Tom Walker, whose running between wickets was likened to 'the rude machinery of a steam-engine in the infancy of construction'.

The royal seal of approval had long been stamped on the playing fields – in the case of Frederick Louis, son of George II, killing field would be more apposite – and patronage had extended from considerable financial support for Surrey to a free dinner at the *Feathers* for Richmond and Brentford teams after a game on the green, courtesy of George III. His brother's death – the result of a ruptured internal abscess caused by a blow from a cricket ball – did not deter the King and Queen Charlotte from celebrating their eldest daughter's birthday in 1798 with a cricket match at Maiden Castle, for which the winning side received a round of beef and a riband.

An early nineteenth-century Continental School watercolour of a cricket match in meadows beneath a European City.

The unfortunate Prince's mishap is a reminder of an ill-conceived hoax at Brook's Club in 1822. A rumour was circulated that the Earl of Hardwicke, while standing beside his daughter, Lady Caledon, at a cricket match, had been struck by a ball and since expired. As is often the way with hearsay the story had gained ample credence before Lord Pollington arrived hot foot with the news that, unlike Polonius, he had just seen the deceased eating a hearty breakfast.

Cricket, whether regal or regular, had a chequered existence between the 1790s and the 1820s. Conflicts with Spain and France diverted manpower to provide cannon-fodder for Admirals of the Fleet, and the sound of gunfire around the shores of Europe supplanted the thwack of bat against ball in the parishes of England. During the hostilities with Napoleon in the Mediterranean and the West Indies, and later throughout the Peninsular campaigns, relatively little really important cricket took place at home.

But even war cannot quell true enthusiasm. If the Duke of Wellington was correct in ascribing victory at Waterloo to the playing fields at Eton he certainly would not have objected to the meeting of officers of different corps at Valenciennes in 1816 whose purpose was to form a Garrison Cricket Club. At that inaugural gathering it was decided that the members play two days each week on the Plain of Mons, that the committee meet every Thursday at Wright's Hotel, Rue de Grand Fossart, that the dress of the Club be white jacket and 'trousers' and, most importantly, that no member might leave a game 'without the unanimous consent of the parties playing and in such case a substitute will be required'. No half measures there.

The listings away from the war zones, however, radiate far less compulsion and consequently are far more compelling. Cricketing venues such as Dandelion Fields, Seven Oaks, Perram Down, Lexdon Heath, Dartford Brimp and Mr. Timothy Drewry's Paddock at the sign of the *Sun* near Gravesend, create an onomatopoeic country rhapsody by comparison, though an intriguing contest between Eleven Gentlemen of St. James and Eleven Gentlemen of Clare Market, one of the most notorious areas in London, brings us back brusquely to the realities of metropolitan existence.

Around the turn of the century, just north of the City, the Homerton Club sprang into prominence and over the next few years attracted many fine players to its ranks. With a couple of exceptions, their names mean little today – Sir

Early nineteenth century print after James Pollard and reproduced in *The Graphic*.

One of the first handbill advertisements for a game at Lord's in 1815, the same year as the Battle of Waterloo.

# CRICKET.

## A GRAND MATCH WILL BE PLAYED
### In LORD's NEW Cricket Ground,
St. JOHN's WOOD MARY-LE-BONE,

On TUESDAY, JUNE the 20th, 1815, and the following day between TWO SELECT ELEVENS of all ENGLAND.

## For One Thousand Guineas a Side.

The WICKETS to be Pitched at ELEVEN o'Clock

PLAYERS,

| | |
|---|---|
| LORD F. BEAUCLERK | Sir T. JONES Bart. |
| Hon. D. KINNAIRD | G. OSBALDESTON Esq. |
| T. MELLISH Esq. | E. H. BUDD Esq. |
| C. MITFORD Esq. | J. PAULETT Esq. |
| — BRAND Esq. | W. WARD Esq. |
| — HOWARD | J. TANNER Esq. |
| — HAMMOND | A. SHABNER Esq. |
| — BELDHAM | — LAMBERT |
| Jas. SHERMAN | H. BENTLEY |
| J. WELLS Junr. | J. BENNETT |
| B. DARK. | — SMALL. |

ADMITTANCE SIX PENCE, GOOD STABLING on the GROUND.
The Cricket Laws, BATS, BALLS, and STUMPS to be had at the Ground or at Mr. LORD's HOUSE in Upper Gloster Street,— the nearest Carriage way is along the New Road through Upper Baker-Street or the Road opposite Mary le-bone Work-house NO DOGS ADMITTED. A MARQUEE to be Let, or SOLD. will Hold 100 PERSONS.

Craft, Printer, Wells-Street, Oxford-Street.

Henry Martin, F. Ladbroke, Holland and Pontifax were all Homerton stalwarts – but their success rate was high and their subsequent obscurity is our misfortune. If Nyren had been granted a longer life we might have learned more of their affairs, as in the introduction to the *locus classicus* Cowden Clarke hints at character studies of a later generation in future editions. Nyren played often for Homerton, sometimes keeping wicket and sometimes being included solely for his batting prowess; witness August 1804, when he scored 65 not out and 36 against the combined forces of Stoke Newington, Hackney and Clapton.

Another who played frequently for Homerton was the jovial wine merchant Benjamin Aislabie, later to become the first secretary of the MCC. Aislabie's great girth drastically reduced his mobility in the field – after he reached 20 stones he was allowed a runner both for batting and fielding – but it says much for the likeability of this 'hippopotamus among greyhounds' that fellow players generously condoned his 'passenger' status. Aislabie had a gift for witty ditties and was delighted when given the chance to entertain; he was also the subject of some verses:

*'Tis Aislabie's boast to form most of the matches*
*In this way at cricket; he makes but few catches,*
*But still he's contented some money to pay*
*For the sake of encouraging excellent play*

*Cricket Match Extraordinary* after Thomas Rowlandson. A blowsy encounter near the Balls Pond Road, Newington in 1811, between eleven women of Hampshire and eleven women of Surrey.

An elongated Zingaro! One of the rules of the I Zingari Club is that 'Zingaric bowlers are requested not to become rubbers of heads, hats, caps etc. when a ball passes accidentally near a wicket.' (See p. 54)

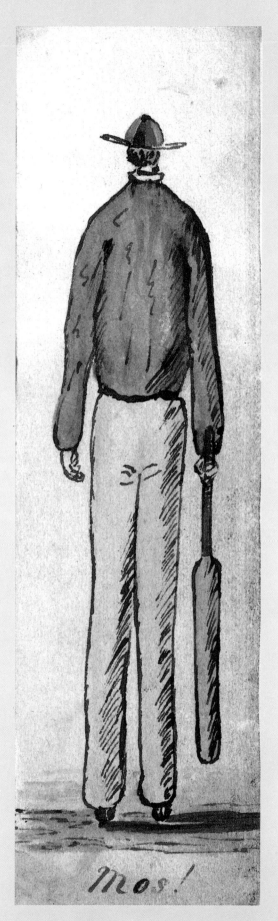

*He doats on the game, has played many a year,*
*Weighs at least seventeen stones, on his pins rather queer;*
*But he still takes the bat, and there's no better fun*
*Than to see him when batting attempting to run.'*

A very different personality from Aislabie was Lord Frederick Beauclerk, who achieved his highest score for Homerton: 170 against Montpelier on Aram's ground at Walworth in 1806. Beauclerk was a son of the Duke of St. Albans and a grandson of Charles II by way of Nell Gwyn. *Lord's and the MCC* by F.S. Ashley-Cooper and Lord Harris, published in 1914, gives the following summary:

'Lord Frederick Beauclerk is the greatest name in the history of the MCC. Not only was he the finest all-round gentleman-player in England for many years, but in matches both great and small his word was law. On the field he was an autocrat – it has been said that his success as a captain was due largely to the fact that no one dared to disobey him – and it was due partly to his great skill as a player that his fellow-members deferred to almost his every wish in matters concerning the Club's policy and welfare. So pre-eminent and well-established was his authority that he might have said with the poet:

*'I am the batsman and the bat*
*I am the bowler and the ball,*
*The umpire, the pavilion cat,*
*The roller, pitch, and stumps, and all'*

The distinguished dramatic critic, Harold Hobson, comparing the records of the all-time greats of cricket, has assessed Beauclerk as equal, if not superior to W.G. Grace. He was one of the most successful batsmen of his day, making eight centuries at Lord's and a 99 for the 'Bs' against England, also a cunning slow bowler who took 66 wickets in 1797, a seasonal record that lasted thirty-four years. It would seem that Beauclerk's single batting weakness was the result of impetuousness, 'that of cutting straight balls – and he has been bowled out in consequence,' says Nyren.

Overall then, there would appear no doubt at all about Lord Fred's due as an outstanding cricketer, but there are many question marks left unresolved with regard to his abuse of power. Stories about his gamesmanship are legion, which draws another comparison with Grace. Beauclerk possessed a volatile temper and could easily be riled. Clever opponents made sure that he often was. Nor was Beauclerk averse to manipulating subordinates into doing things his way even if that meant interfering with the running of the game. Bentley, the MCC scorer, had to contend with many uncomfortable moments. As captain, Beauclerk would sometimes keep himself on for too long in the hope of eventually capturing a wicket:

'Do you not think it time for a change?' some bold soul would meekly ask.

'Certainly,' Beauclerk would reply, 'I'll change ends.'

His arrogance even extended to hanging a valuable gold watch by its chain from the middle stump and contemptuously defying any bowler to hit it, though he was careful to choose an unpenetrative attack before risking the timepiece.

He reckoned to make six hundred pounds a year from cricket, a not-so-modest sum to add to his stipend as vicar of St. Albans, where occasionally, very occasionally, he would be found giving a sermon from a saddle in the pulpit. The saddle was always there, but Beauclerk mostly was not, 'ne'er preached once of a twelvemonth', was the condemnatory comment of one of his congregation.

(*Top*) The Rev. Lord Frederick Beauclerk, who attracted thousands of spectators whenever he played. He dominated cricket fields with supreme generalship for thirty years. Harold Hobson has written of Beauclerk: 'All the time that England was beating Napoleon – and we weren't very quick on that particular job – his reputation was known all over the country. He was batting and bowling in first-class cricket before Bonaparte had been heard of. He was batting and bowling ten years later still, when Napoleon was routed at Waterloo; and five years after that, when Napolen was dying at St. Helena, he was batting and bowling as well as ever.' He was the first bowler in England ever to use sawdust to get a better grip on a wet ball.

(*Bottom*) George 'Squire' Osbaldeston, who undoubtedly qualifies as one of the greatest all-round sportsmen of the nineteenth century. As a Lt. Colonel of local militia during the Napoleonic Wars, Osbaldeston was reprimanded for organizing sack races instead of drill.

(*Next page*) This is the attractively coloured lithograph, pirated by S. Lipschitz, of perhaps the most popular cricket print of any age. *A Cricket Match between Sussex and Kent* was issued by W.H. Mason, who usually concentrated on marine subjects, and is an amalgam of players who took part in the fixture between 1849 and 1851. It also includes 'many Noblemen and Gentlemen, Patrons of the Noble Game of Cricket', to quote the accompanying prospectus. The original Mason copperplate engraving contained a central gap between the foreground figures.

The ignoble Lord had other character defects. An anecdote told to Frederick Gale by the old Mitcham cricketer, John Bowyer, revealed a considerable selfishness and greed:

'. . . in a match, when a noble lord drew himself in the guinea lottery for runs, and was in with him (Bowyer), he would not run any runs hardly but his own if he could help it, in order to get the lottery . . . I call that kind of thing which Lord ———— did "cheating" and nothing more or less.'

A round-arm delivery à la Christina Willes. S. T. Dodd's illustration.

Whatever one thinks of Beauclerk it is well to judge his actions in the context of the times. Lord's was inhabited by 'men with book and pencil, betting as openly and professionally as in the ring at Epsom and ready to deal in the odds with any and every person of speculative propensities . . . Jim and Joe Bland, of turf notoriety, with Dick Whitlom of Covent Garden, Simpson, a gaming-house keeper, and Toll of Esher, attended as regularly at Lord's as Crockford and Gully at Epsom and Ascot; and the idea that all the Surrey and Hampshire rustics should either want or resist strong temptations to sell, is not to be entertained for a moment. The constant habit of betting will take the honesty out of any man.' The words of another man of the cloth, the Rev. James Pycroft.

We will never know how many catches were deliberately dropped, how many balls carefully missed. All sorts of skullduggery was practised in the dingy London taverns patronized by 'sportsmen'; insidious whispers of supposed deceits by fellow players dispelling the doubts of those thought open to persuasion. 'One artifice,' said William Ward, MP, who made the first recorded individual score over 200 in 1820, 'was to keep a player out of the way by a false report that his wife was dead'; a particularly despicable example of a number of unpleasant ruses used to keep the hucksters happy and their money safe.

William Lambert, of the brilliant eye and quickness of movement, a leading all-round player of his day, was once accused of 'selling a match'. At a later date he became involved in an argument in front of the pavilion at Lord's. Angry voices were raised, accusations and counter-accusations made, a crowd gathered and the authorities sitting within earshot *in sanctorum* were left with no alternative but to conduct an enquiry. None other than the darker-shade-of-pale Lord Fred led the enquiry – or was it an inquisition? Lambert, who, seven years before, in 1810, had taken his own as well as the unfit 'Squire' Osbaldeston's place in a contest against Beauclerk and Howard and won the day, much to the umbrage of the aristocratic cleric, found an unchristian lack of forgiveness. He was banned from Lord's forever.

It was not often that George Osbaldeston failed to come up to the mark. He surely qualifies as one of the greatest nineteenth-century achievers. A brilliant rider to hounds, he also bestrode a horse in every classic, beat the French and Italian Real Tennis champions using only his gloved hand, won several boxing bouts when conceding up to four stones, was an outstanding marksman and athlete, took ten wickets in an innings and won a match at Lord's whilst sustaining a broken shoulder. As if that were not enough Osbaldeston won a wager for 1,000 guineas to ride 200 miles in ten hours. He finished with seventy-eight minutes in hand, having mounted 27 horses. At the age of 66 he went 72 hours without sleep in a marathon of billiards and racing, and in his 80th year, just before he died, while suffering from gout and confined to a bathchair, won a bet for a sovereign that he could not sit for a day without moving. A competitor to the last.

A contemporary of the 'Squire of England', as Osbaldeston was tagged, and another leading figure of early nineteenth-century cricket was Edward Hayward Budd. Budd was a tremendous smiter of the ball: 'I used to delight in hard hitting, and in seeing the ring obliged to fall back further and further as I warmed in my play. To step into an over-pitched ball, and drive with all the impetus of my heavy bat, weighing three pounds of good stuff, was my favourite play.'

Budd twice hit a ball for nine (boundaries were yet to be introduced), at Woolwich and at Sevenoaks, and in a match between Surrey and England at Lord's in 1808 drove a delivery right out of the ground and through the glass

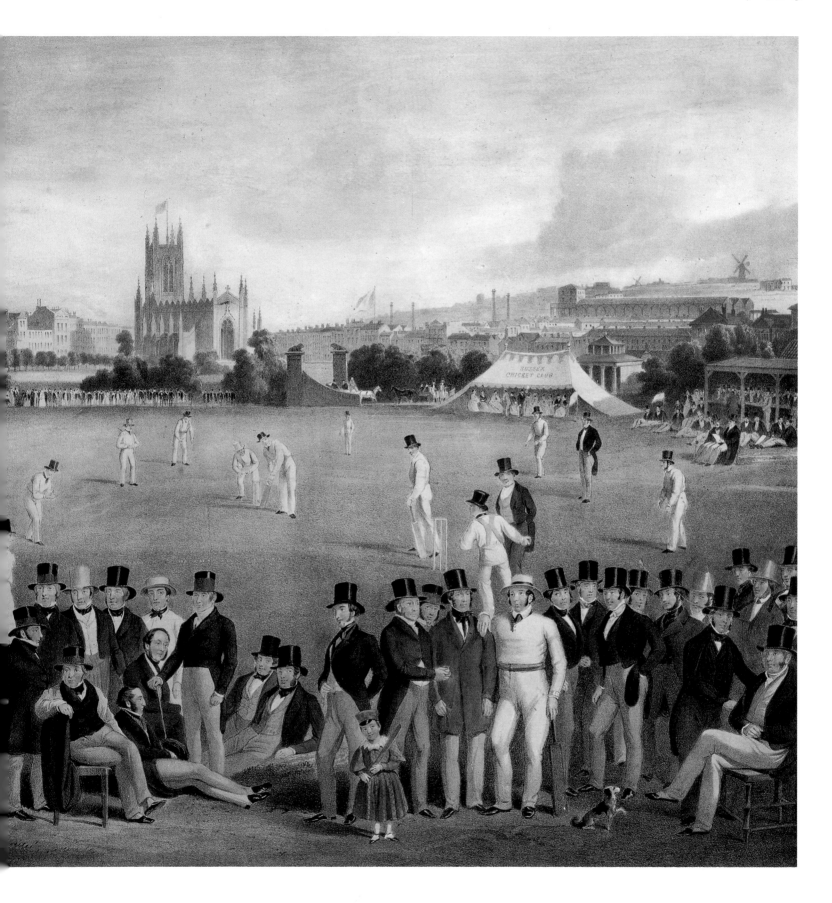

of a greenhouse. 'Silver Billy' Beldham recalled the occasion. 'Lord had said he would forfeit twenty-five guineas (actually, the figure was twenty) if anyone thus proved his ground too small: so we all crowded around Mr. Budd and told him what he might claim. "Well then," he said, "I claim it, and give it among the players."' The claim was not acknowledged, however, and the eager participants were unable to get their hands on the booty. It would appear that Thomas Lord's renowned business acumen had fostered a convenient memory.

Budd was also a fine bowler, wicket-keeper and fielder. In a game at Nottingham in 1817 between twenty-two of that City and England he made nine catches; he was respected as a fast-moving mid-wicket. His bowling technique consisted of delivering the ball from the hip at medium pace 'sort of half-round-armed, with his hand slightly extended from his side'; it enabled him to impart spin and to get the ball to rise sharply.

Thus began the transition from ground-level or low underarm bowling to round-arm *en route* to the eventual practice of overarm. Inevitably there was fierce opposition at each stage of modernization.

'About the year 1818 Lambert and I,' said Budd, 'attained to a kind of round-arm delivery, by which we rose decidedly superior to all the batsmen of the day. Mr. Ward could not play it, but he headed a party against us, and our new bowling was ignored.'

By the time Budd reached his eighties and was living in contented retirement in Wiltshire, surrounded by a virtual zoo of pets – canine, ovine, bovine and porcine – and twenty thousand tulips, round-arm had in turn been replaced by the newly legalized overarm. Ignoring a development did not make it go away.

The idea for round-arm bowling has been attributed variously to Tom Walker of Hambledon, David Harris of the same club, William Ashby, Mrs. Lambert and/or Mrs. and Miss Christina Willes of Fonford. Whomever, it would seem that at some time or another a lady bowled in a wide arc to avoid brushing against her hooped skirts, and the possible advantages of such an attack were realized.

Whatever doubt surrounds the birth of the new 'form' there was absolutely

# Cricket.

## A MATCH WILL BE PLAYED,

### IN THE

## LONDON FIELDS, HACKNEY,

On THURSDAY, SEPTEMBER 14th, 1815,

*Between eleven Gentlemen of*

# The Ratcliff Cricket Club,

### AND ELEVEN GENTLEMEN OF THE

## LONDON CRICKET CLUB,

### FOR FIFTY GUINEAS A SIDE.

*The Wickets to be pitched at Ten o' Clock.*

Another early handbill.

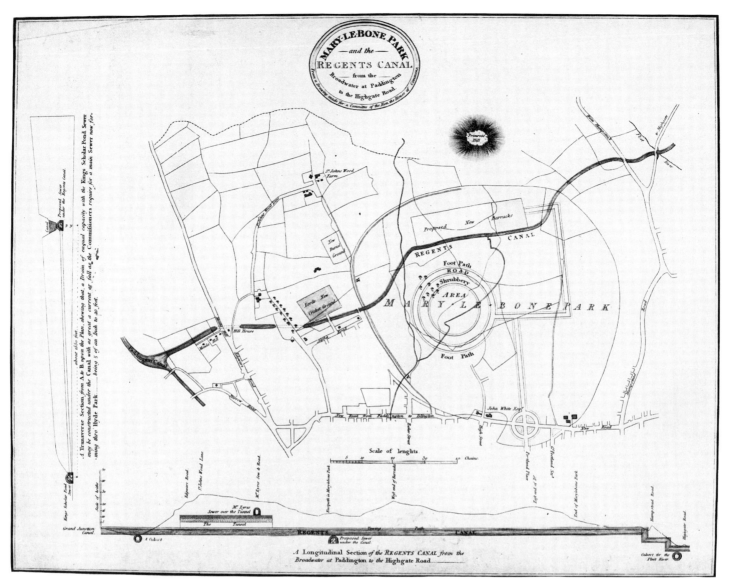

Map showing Lord's second ground. Roughly situated where Warsop's the bat-makers once had premises and the Marylebone railway sidings now exist.

no question that John Willes, Christina's brother, became a leading advocate. Many times in rural matches away from the eyes of the cricket authorities he would persevere with the round-arm mode, often in the face of uproar and con-fusion as stumps were drawn by disenchanted opponents. The showdown had to come, and it came as if pre-destined, at Lord's.

Opening the bowling for Kent against MCC in 1822, Willes sent down a round-arm delivery and was immediately no-balled. He threw the ball down in fury, stalked off to his horse and rode away somewhat theatrically into the distance. Willes never played cricket again at a reported level.

The reactionary William Ward, who had so strongly denounced round-arm, was soon to be hailed at headquarters as the saviour of cricket. Ward had been born in Islington in 1787, the very year that the cricketing élite deserted the district to go west. He worked as a banker in Antwerp, joined a partnership with his father and at the tender age of thirty was elected a Director of the Bank of England. In 1826 he became the Tory member of Parliament for the City of London and more than two score years after that he produced a book on monetary legislation.

Ward's heyday as a cricketer was in the 1820s. A tall loose-limbed rather pre-occupied looking man, he had a predilection for heavy bats; in fact the same four-pound willow accounted for all his major scores including, as we have seen, the highest ever made at Lord's. His remarkable 278, a record for the ground until 1925, demonstrates enviable concentration over a long period. Even so, perhaps his mind was on weightier matters than cricket, for after a game in which he had been dismissed for 42 and 20 he was heard to declare that 'he should have made more in the second innings had he not been thinking of a coming Corn Law debate'.

Before examining Ward's act of rescue it is worth remembering that by the time he came into the picture Lord's had moved twice. During the early 1800s London was expanding and the price of new property rising. The lease of the first ground at Dorset Square was close to expiry in 1808 and so Thomas Lord wisely rented from Henry Samuel Eyre two fields called Brick and Great a little farther north. Shortly before this Edward Berkeley Portman, owner of the estate encompassing Dorset Square, had tried to negotiate a new lease at a greatly increased premium. Lord would not agree, and went ahead with his contingency plan. But it was not until 1813 that the Marylebone Club started to play on the 'same footing' (Lord had taken the turf with him) in new surroundings. In the interim the North Bank ground, as it came to be called, was used by the St. John's Wood Cricket Club. Dorset Square finally closed for cricket in 1811 and so for two seasons Marylebone played no fixtures 'at home'. The only event of significance in that time had been an anniversary dinner in quarters by 'the carriage-way up Lisson Grove, opposite the *Yorkshire Stingo*'. The '*Stingo*' was a tea-house, not a tavern, and conceivably did not hold much attraction for thirsty cricketers, who preferred a stronger brew. At any rate only three games were played at the second ground by the MCC during their tenure, and had it not been for another forced move yet farther north the club might well have foundered.

The extension of the Grand Junction Canal from Paddington Basin formed part of John Nash's design for the northern boundary of the Regent's Park. Lord first heard of the plan in 1812 and realized it would cut a swathe through his cricket field, so having chiselled £4,000 compensation from the landowners he again picked up his turf and walked. The *new* new ground was on farmland very close to Punker's Barn, or Red Barn as it was sometimes called, and the duck-pond that was on the spot was forever to cause drainage problems for generations of groundsmen. At last, however, Lord had found a permanent home for the club.

His troubles though, were not over. There was an explosion, caused by the careless use of gunpowder, in a public house beside the cricket field mere days before the planned auspicious opening, which somewhat took the gloss from the occasion.

It is in 1825 that we rejoin William Ward. Lord was getting old and looking for security. He was also experiencing financial difficulties and so obtained permission to have erected seven pairs of houses on the ground. Alarmed members got to hear of the proposed sale and approached Ward, who in turn approached Lord.

'It's said you are going to sell us,' he remarked. The affirmative reply was qualified only by the obtainable price. 'What are you asking?' enquired Ward. '£5,000,' answered Lord. 'Give me pen and ink,' the banker demanded.

No sooner had Ward taken possession than disaster struck. The *Morning Post* of Saturday, July 30, 1825, relayed the sorry tale:

(*Right*) The multi-coloured match card for the centenary match of the present ground.

One of a number of matches at various times between disabled pensioners, that attracted large crowds.

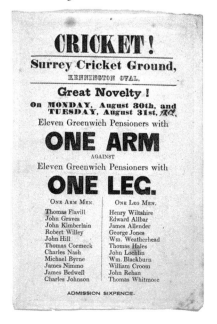

## LORD'S CRICKET GROUND CENTENARY

1814    1851    1885

1814    1914

### LORD'S GROUND.

### M.C.C. v. HERTFORDSHIRE,
#### JUNE 22nd, 1814.

| 1st Innings. | HERTFORDSHIRE. | 2nd Innings. | |
|---|---|---|---|
| Mowbray, c Ward | 4 | b Beauclerk | 1 |
| H. Bentley, not out | 33 | run out | 0 |
| Bruton, b Budd | 7 | b Osbaldeston | 17 |
| S. Carter, b Budd | 0 | st Vigne | 0 |
| Sibley, b Beauclerk | 6 | c Budd | 1 |
| Taylor, c Beauclerk | 6 | run out | 2 |
| Denham, b Budd | 10 | st Vigne | 21 |
| T. Carter, b Budd | 1 | b Osbaldeston | 0 |
| J. Sibley, c Beauclerk | 6 | not out | 3 |
| Freeman, c Beauclerk | 2 | run out | 5 |
| Crew, b Beauclerk | 0 | st Vigne | 0 |
| Byes | 4 | Byes | 5 |
| Total | 79 | Total | 55 |

M.C.C.

| | |
|---|---|
| Mr. A. Schabner, c J. Sibley | 55 |
| Hon. D. Kinnaird, b S. Carter | 1 |
| Mr. C. Warren, b Taylor | 25 |
| Mr. E. H. Budd, c T. Carter | 36 |
| Hon. E. Bligh, b Bentley | 6 |
| Mr. T. Burgoyne, run out | 0 |
| Lord F. Beauclerk, b Taylor | 3 |
| Mr. G. Osbaldeston, b Mowbray | 18 |
| Mr. W. Ward, run out | 10 |
| Mr. T. Vigne, b Bentley | 2 |
| Mr. J. Poulet, not out | 1 |
| Byes | 4 |
| Total | 161 |

## DESTRUCTION OF THE ASSEMBLY, BETTING, AND DRESSING ROOMS AT LORD'S CRICKET GROUNDS

*About one o'clock yesterday morning a fire was discovered in the above ornamental buildings, attached to the far-famed grounds belonging formerly to Mr. Lord (but now in the possession of a Mr. Ward) in which, perhaps, some of the greatest cricketers have played and alternatively won and lost thousands.*

Fire engines from as far afield as Poplar, to the east of the City, failed to quench the blaze; there was no on-site supply of water and within hours there remained only a smouldering ruin. The greatest catastrophe of all was that the irreplaceable records and trophies of early cricket had been completely destroyed.

Ten years later Ward transferred the lease of the ground to James Henry Dark for £2,000 and an annuity of £425. The Dark era, paradoxically, was full of light, for he proved an assiduous caretaker and made many splendid improvements to facilities at Lord's.

Another generation of cricketers were now making their presence felt. Prominent among the bowlers was Frederick William Lillywhite, who with Jem Broadbridge had bowled Sussex to victory against England in two of the three trial matches designed to test the fairness of the round-arm method. Lillywhite had not appeared in a recorded important game until he reached the advanced age of 30, yet for two to three decades from the mid-20s he was seldom out of the record lists. The 'Nonpareil', as he was known, was one of the most relentlessly accurate slow-medium bowlers of all time, in his entire career reputed never to have bowled more than a half-dozen wides. In 1831 he took 77 wickets in front rank matches, and six years later became the first to exceed 100 in such games, finishing the season on 120. In 1840 he went farther and reached 133, then in 1842 totalled 157.

That indefatigable cricketing archivist, Arthur Haygarth, compared Lillywhite with 'a piece of machinery, seldom out of order and in his old age only wanted a little oiling, when he would have been as effective as ever'.

Around 1830 Kentish cricket came once more into its own, a renaissance due chiefly to two players, Alfred Mynn and Fuller Pilch. Pilch arrived in the county with a reputation nurtured in Norfolk, but Mynn was a true son of the Weald, having been born in Goudhurst, near Tunbridge Wells. Massively built, he was a naturally powerful hitter and fast round-arm bowler of great stamina. Frederick Gale described his approach to the wicket: 'Alfred Mynn walked six steps exactly, in the last step accelerating his pace and landing heavily on his left foot, so heavily that if the ground was soft, he dug a grave almost, as his trained weight without an ounce of flesh was 17 stone'. He was once asked for an opinion on the right number of balls to constitute an over. In Porthos-like manner, he replied: 'For myself, I should like 100 balls to the over'.

Mynn's colleague in the county side, Fuller Pilch, was regarded as the most commanding batsman of his time. His Kentish career ran from 1836 to 1854 and he won a great number of matches by his devastating attack, in which 'he seemed to crush the best bowling by his long forward plunge before it had time to shoot, to rise, or do mischief by catches'. Pilch had an agreement by which he received £100 per annum for his endeavours, no mean sum in those days, and his worth to Kent is shown by the fact that after he retired they experienced a succession of defeats for several seasons.

(*Right*) A woodcut from *An Almanac of Twelve Sports* by Sir William Newzam Prior Nicholson, that was published in 1898 with accompanying verses from Rudyard Kipling:

*Thank God who made the British Isles
And taught me how to play,
I do not worship crocodiles
Or bow the knee to clay!*

*Give me a willow wand and I,
With hide and cork and twine,
From century to century
Will gambol round my Shrine.*

Nicholson produced a series of woodcut illustrated books and won renown as a portrait artist and stage scenery and costume designer. The batsman in this illustration is surely meant to be Alfred Mynn, champion cricketer of England in the middle years of the nineteenth century.

The purpose of this match was twofold. Two years before, Mynn had gone to prison for unpaid debts and it was hoped the receipts would enable him to reach a more secure financial footing. Equally, it was to publicly display the affection with which Mynn was held throughout the country.

Admission
TO THE TESTIMONIAL IN HONOR OF
**A. MYNN, Esq.**
AT LORDS, JULY 26th & 27th, 1847,
Patronized by
THE MARYLEBONE CLUB.
Match—Between Two Select ELEVENS of all England.

The Mynn's, Pilch's and fellow players were able to contemplate a period of great change in these central years of cricket's evolution, and not only on the field. As might be expected, laws had been amended and altered, often reluctantly, in response to experiment and refinement. The length of the bat was limited to 38 inches after 1835, the follow-on was compulsory after a deficit of 100 runs, reduced to 80 in 1854, and the circumference of the ball was established at between 9 and $9\frac{1}{4}$ inches in 1838. But it was the onset of the industrial revolution, in particular the spread of the railway system to new urban and old rural communities that so altered the perspective of the game.

Mynn, who in 1836 had endured a hundred-mile-plus journey from Leicester to St. Bartholomew's Hospital in London, strapped to a stagecoach roof after a serious ankle injury, would a few years later have been able to get to the surgeon much more quickly and comfortably under steam. Fortunately the 'Lion of Kent' persuaded the physicians not to amputate the limb and two years later was once more pulverising the turf.

With machinery helping the missionaries of the game to spread its gospel there remained some endearing anomalies. Around 1850 mowing machines were put to use for cutting grass in several areas, but at Lord's they stayed loyal to the mutton-munchers. Sir Spencer Ponsonby-Fane, later Honorary Treasurer of MCC and moving force in the acquisition of their picture collection, never forgot the scene:

> *The grass was never mowed. It was usually kept down by a flock of sheep which was penned-up on match-days, and on Saturdays four or five hundred sheep were driven on to the ground on their way to the Monday Smithfield Market. It was marvellous to see how they cleared the herbage.*

Ponsonby-Fane, his brother Lord Bessborough, John Loraine Baldwin and R.P. Long were responsible for founding one of the earliest of the wandering clubs I Zingari. 'The Gypsies', to translate, were formed in 1845 and maintained selective membership, one of their rules being 'that the entrance be nothing, and that the annual subscription do not exceed the entrance'. IZ were a force with which to be reckoned, and forged a link with the renowned Canterbury Cricket Week, where they participated in theatricals and other entertainments that complemented the cricket games.

A song of the time, to the tune of 'Rule Britannia', had a second verse that went:

> *The Marylebone ranks first of all,*
> *It's they who do our laws enrol;*
> *And then I Zingari, those trumps with bat and ball,*
> *And the Eleven of All-England, composed of great and small.*

The man who made the song his own was a one-eyed bricklayer called William Clarke. It could be argued that Clarke was more influential in developing cricket than any other one person. Apart from his playing ability – several thousands of wickets in a top-class career of over forty years – it was he who turned a Nottingham meadow into Trent Bridge cricket ground and crucially, in 1846, instituted the All-England Cricket Club. The XI travelled to all corners of the country – remote areas that had never before seen major cricketers – playing local XVs, XVIIIs and XXIIs for a guarantee of gate money. Clarke kept tight control on all aspects of the operation, being manager, captain and leading bowler. He once told Pycroft, of *Cricket Field* fame: 'It is going to be, sir, from

(*Top*) A belt buckle showing a somewhat unrealistic catch at the wicket.

(*Centre*) A catastrophic run out is imminent. Brass clasp depicting two batsmen colliding.

(*Bottom*) The brass clasp is decorated with the names of the second English side to visit Australia, 1863–4.

A cricket match played 25 July, 1857 at Hundonsbury, the seat of E. P. Calvert, Esq., between the Royal Artillery and the Hundonsbury Club. Roger Fenton's photograph is likely to be the earliest still extant of a cricketing engagement.

one end of the land to the other; it will make good for cricket – it will make good for you as well as me.' It certainly made good for Clarke. He earned a lot of money, in fact a fortune. His players received not quite so much – anything from fifty shillings to six pounds in later years, according to status and performance. Some of them did not like the financial arrangements or Clarke's attitude. He was caustic and tyrannical and they rebelled.

Thus was Clarke's monopoly broken. The success of the All-England XI spawned imitators who inevitably became competitors. Soon a whole array of itinerant elevens were criss-crossing the land, not all at the same time but in sufficient numbers thereof to make the good for the greater whole.

Not every one of Clarke's cricketers disliked him. The President of the AEE (All-England Eleven) was Nicholas Felix, or Wanostrocht, to give his real name, and he it was who wrote supportive letters to the press when Clarke was being berated in the columns of *Bell's Life* for 'niggardly dealings'. Felix, in 1852, produced a pamphlet entitled *How to play Clarke*, perhaps belatedly laughing at himself for the occasion seven years before when he had jauntily taken guard four yards in front of the wicket only to be bowled for a duck by the wily William. Clarke had taken sixteen wickets in that match for Nottinghamshire v Kent, gaining 'twist and life from the pitch by spinning the ball out high from under his arm-pit'.

Felix was a remarkable and delightful character – a full coverage of his life and doings can be found in several of Gerald Brodribb's splendid *œuvres* – and he refuses to be conveniently categorized. A schoolmaster by profession and a writer, he possessed a seemingly endless aggregation of attributes. In *The History of Kent Cricket*, he is described as 'a most gifted man, being a fine conversationalist, artist, musician – for some years he conducted the band at the theatre during the Canterbury Week – singer, linguist, all-round sportsman

The first match on the first tour by an English side to Australia. H.H. Stephenson's XI finding their land-legs against a Victorian 18 at Melbourne on New Year's Day, 1862.

and inventor of the catapulta; he also originated the tubular india-rubber gloves, and gave the invention to William Caldccourt of Lord's. After playing cricket all day in the Canterbury Week, he has been known to play the violin in the orchestra at the theatre and also dance a *pas de deux* on the stage with Mr. C. Morse.'

As Nicholas Felix, who gave of his talents so munificently, declined into ill health and penury his *diminuendo* was contrasted by a *crescendo* of cricketing activity. The game had reached another staging-post. The huge stakes of early years had long disappeared, and had, one suspects, for most of its latter term been merely nominal amounts paraded to boost the importance of the occasion. In other words, no money actually changed hands whatever the result. The betting in the crowd and between team individuals had continued unabated, of course, for much longer, but even that had gone once the playing of some sports, especially cricket, had become inculcated with a high moral tone.

As the 1850s stretched towards the '60s and '70s, representative tours began to take place; a county championship started to become established; annuals, guides and correlated literature jostled for a place on the bookstalls; products with cricket as a theme arrived in the market-place and the red dye from the ball marked trousers worldwide.

Much had happened and much was still to happen, some of it prosaic, some prestigious. A Commander-in-Chief of the Army had ordered cricket grounds to be made near every barracks in the kingdom; a bowler, William Hillyer of Kent, had become the first to exceed 200 wickets in important matches during a season; a side at Ware, losing to neighbouring Hertford, had burnt their gear and given up the game; and for the first time a hat had been awarded, to Stephenson, the Surrey professional, for taking three wickets in successive balls.

Cricket had reached maturity, and come of age. What lay ahead?

THE MOTHER EARTH WORM TO IT'S WORMLET :— —— NOW THEN FLORIZEL, THAT JUST SERVES YOU RIGHT,— HOW OFTEN HAVE I TOLD YOU TO KEEP AWAY FROM THE WICKET DURING THESE TEST MATCHES,

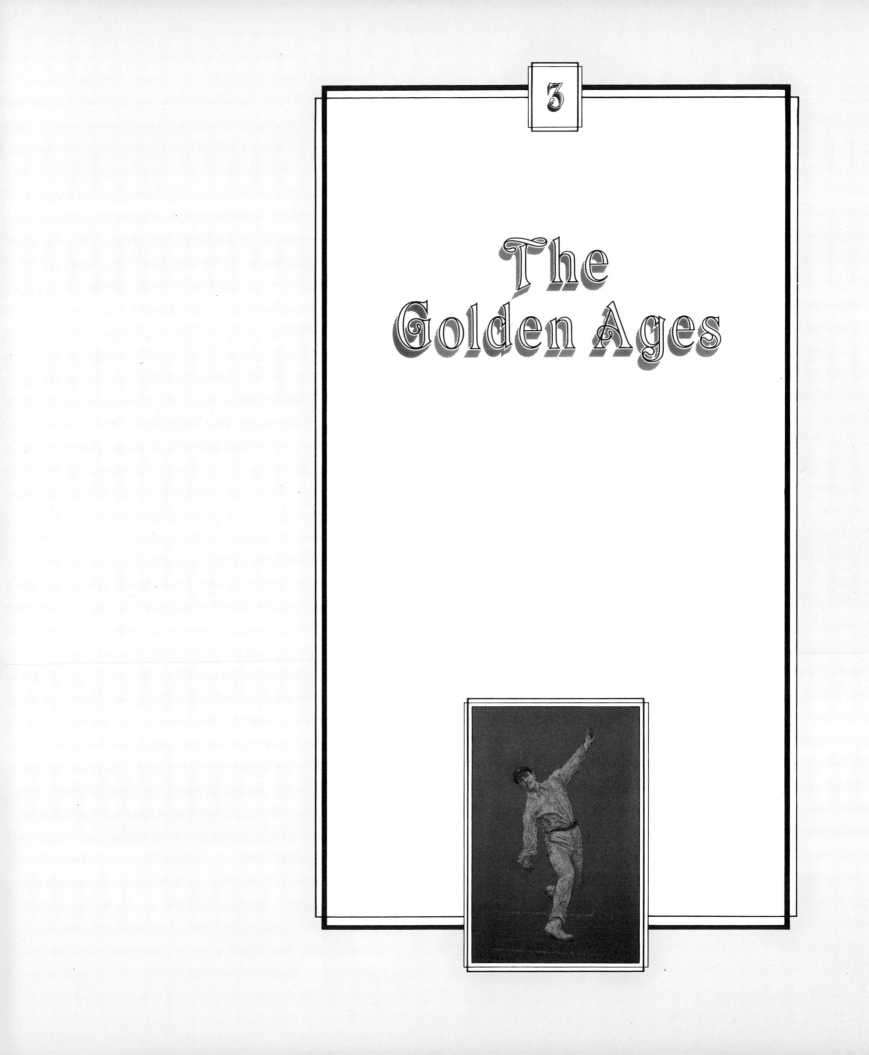

# The Golden Ages

3

(*Previous page*) The mother earthworm to its wormlet: '*How then Florizel, that just serves you right. How often have I told you to keep away from the wicket during these Test Matches?*' William Heath Robinson, 1872–1944. Pen, ink, watercolour and bodycolour.

A set of fourteen pin-back badges, each depicting a member of the England team to Australia, 1897–98. The cameo buttons were mounted on card and issued by the American Tobacco Co.

'Cricket is an idea of the Gods,' wrote J.M. Barrie, when all Victorians knew intuitively that *their* God was an Englishman. The game became part of the social fabric, an arm of what has since been called muscular Christianity, and was ferried with missionary zeal to wherever the Imperial pink had spread on the map. This ethos – a form of Englishry – carried on throughout the Golden Age of the Edwardians and, if dented somewhat by World War I, survived more or less intact through the High Noon between Kaiser Bill and Fuehrer Adolf.

The proud state had been reached but gradually. As the nineteenth century progressed the sharper practices circling the outfield had slipped away and made room for the ideologies of the public school. A succession of visionary schoolmasters – Edward Thring of Uppingham and Edward Bowen of Harrow were prime exemplars – had indoctrinated generations of pupils with the principles of fair play. Compulsory cricket, a form of anti-intellectualism, was commonplace in the groves of Academe and never more apparent than in W.N. Roe's Review of Uppingham, on a typical summer's day when he saw 'eighteen simultaneous games on one ground'.

The concept, ineluctably, stretched back into childhood years. The beguiling tales and poetry of juvenilia, even as early as the 1820s, were transparently extolling the virtues of cricket for young minds of both sexes: for instance, Mrs. Danvers' and Ellen's visit to the cricket field in *Tales of Ellen* and *The Troubles of Harry Careless, or Going Too Far*, whose title leaves little doubt as to its message. From that time on religious tracts had pointed the way to a proverbially straight and narrow path for readers of all ages. Headings such as *Your innings*, or *Life's cricket* and *He did it for me*, brook no indagation and are a reminder of a certain Doctor of Divinity called Parr who, pulling on his pipe and supping from a jug of ale, would sit on the green at Halton, in Warwickshire, on Sunday afternoons watching his parish lads play the game. Those who had not attended church in the morning were not allowed to take part. The supreme archetype of the moral crusader at the crease was the Eton, Cambridge, Middlesex and England batsman C.T. Studd, who became a missionary in China, India and the Belgian Congo. When Studd helped build a church in the Congo he made sure that the aisle was exactly 22 yards. To know that 'Banjo Bwana', as he was called, was addicted to morphine and deserted his wife and children for 'the cause of Christ', reduces the hagiography but somehow strangely

(*Next page left*) Scenes from a Canterbury Cricket Week.

(*Next page right*) Cartoon of one-time secretary to M.C.C., R.A. Fitzgerald, sporting his I Zingari colours (see p. 76).

# CANTERBURY CRICKET WEEK

The Ladies' Corner

ARRIS. GILBERT

A happy Innovation
but hardly into smooth
working order)

A Good Catch

(Mrs Match Hunter
notes so)

'Bob'

Canterbury Belles

"well Sarge what do ee
think o' crickets

*Fitz:*

OUR CRICKETING GUESTS

The Australian and Philadelphian teams, 1884 *The Boy's Own Paper*.

enhances the subject: the remarkable Studd was, after all, vulnerable.

Soon after Frederick Lillywhite left John Wisden on his own to mind the cricket and cigar business in New Coventry Street the boom began. Cricket invariably apes its social clime even if, on occasion, its response is similar to that of the fabled tortoise; in this instance, though, the two were hand-in-glove straight away. Britain was changing rapidly, enjoying great economic growth and importing an enormous range of raw materials which were then manufactured and exported. For a period, an estimated seventy per cent of commodities in the world market was British. The resulting financial confidence that allowed wider suffrage, a new education bill and the availability of more leisure time gave cricket a suitable ambience in which to flourish. An expansion in schooling fostered a general spread of literacy and encouraged the proliferation of reading matter. The newly-arrived and relatively affluent middle-classes and their working-class counterparts, indistinguishable photogenically before the arrival of the cloth cap at the end of the century, thereby became more immediately aware of what was happening to cricket at large. A weekly journal called

(*Next page left*) Over the years cigarette cards have presented a fine pictorial record of cricketers. Some early cards displaying the game's players were issued in the mid-1890s by Marcus, and Messrs. W.D. and H.O. Wills. Many other firms subsequently copied the successful format.

(*Next page right*) With love and for money.

An English School watercolour of a cricket match in India, *c.* 1857 (see p. 125).

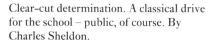

Clear-cut determination. A classical drive for the school – public, of course. By Charles Sheldon.

*The Cricketer* started off in 1869 but fell at the first fence with a single issue; competitors arrived soon after and lasted longer, some of them much longer. W.F. Mandle, writing from the other side of the world at Canberra College of Advanced Education, has estimated that sporting magazines and journals alone grew from fourteen titles in the 1860s to twenty-eight in the 1870s, thirty-four in the 1880s and eighty-seven in the 1890s. The general awareness that the written word created was reflected in all sorts of accoutrements and ornaments with cricketing themes that started to appear: Staffordshire figures, Doulton jugs, ceramics, presentation plates, bronze busts, 'Spy' cartoons, children's games, silver-ware, glass bottles, trophies, cigarette cards, cut-out scraps, pub signs, matchbox labels, belt buckles and beer mats. Beside all these, of course, ran the higher-profile forms of artistic representation that had shown cricketers and their game for a very long time: oil paintings, lithographs, sculptures and woodcuts. Firms eager to promote their wares were not slow to cash in on the perception of cricket as a wholesome activity; practically anything, from embrocation to strong spirits, was judged more marketable with the aid of a cricketing motif. Even a masonic lodge seems to have decided that a crest depicting crossed bats conformed to their aspirations.

Photography too made advances, notably in the work of G.W. Beldam; posed action shots and group studies reproduced on postcards proving a popular purchase for members of the cricketing public. Coloured drawings by political satirists, and at a level of general buffoonery, were also produced. For example, the caption 'Thornton carried his bat, how do you carry yours?' accompanied a skilful sketch of a small figure laden with an over-size one; or a ball being smashed through a kitchen window by a portly adult playing with youngsters in the backyard had the line: 'Uncle Podger shows the children how to play cricket'. More subtle humorous delineations were often the work of Donald McGill and later Tom Browne, and series portraying cricket and other sports were merchandized by, among others, the business concern, Raphael Tuck, who were renowned for their high-quality product. Cricket also provided the theme for mail of a sentimental or celebratory nature, such as valentines and birthday cards.

Very soon there was enough trove under the loose heading of 'cricketana', to trigger the acquisitive juices of would-be collectors. Not that serious aspirants were likely to remain in a state of 'future indicative' for long; mostly desire led to acquisition with scarcely a pause and, as any of the fraternity in thrall will readily testify, a collection once started rapidly accumulates.

From around the time of the birth of Wisden's Almanack to the present there have been some legendary collectors of cricketing artefacts. Among the first, who specialized in books, written ephemera and pictures, was the naturalized

PLAYER'S CIGARETTES

P. G. H. FENDER
(SURREY)

PLAYER'S CIGARETTES

F. E. WOOLLEY
(KENT)

PLAYER'S CIGARETTES

A. W. WELLARD
(SOMERSET)

PLAYER'S CIGARETTES

A. P. F. CHAPMAN
(KENT)

PLAYER'S CIGARETTES

K. S. DULEEPSINHJI
(SUSSEX)

PLAYER'S CIGARETTES

M. LEYLAND
(YORKSHIRE)

PLAYER'S CIGARETTES

S.A.C.A.

D. G. BRADMAN

BACHELOR GIRL'S CLUB

A happy New-Year.

Amid'st your harmless games and fun,
Remember that you're Papa's Son,
Obey him there, and guard your wicket,
And you will be a don at Cricket.

Johnny Walker.    Cricketer. 1820.

The SPORTSMAN FOR CRICKET NEWS

FRY'S THE OUTDOOR MAGAZINE.

EDITED BY C.B. FRY.

Huntley & Palmers. Reading & London. BISCUITS.

The National Game—a Sketch in the heart of London!

Pots and pans put to good use on waste land in London a hundred years ago.

Yorkshireman, the Rev. R.S. Holmes. In 1906 Holmes received a letter from another who had amassed a huge collection, A.D. Taylor, the bibliographer, in which Taylor commented: 'I have no hesitation in declaring that you have the most complete cricket library in existence.' Many more over the years have owned or own large and/or selective collections; A.L. Ford, Thomas Padwick, Charles Pratt Green, the polymath F.S. Ashley-Cooper, Rockley Wilson, J.W. Goldman, G. Neville Weston, John Arlott, Anthony Winder, Geoffrey Copinger and David Frith. Anyone wishing to delve more deeply into the lives and habits of the early 'giants in the field' could do no better than read Irving Rosenwater's invaluable essay, *Cricket Books: Great Collectors of the Past*.

A unique aspect of Pratt Green's hobby was his congregation of historic cricket bats, which included those used by many of the leading cricketers up to the outbreak of World War I. At one time he possessed 151 bats, 119 of which were listed in the catalogue of a bazaar held in aid of the County Club at Worcester in 1903. The catalogue brings to mind the refinements sought and found for the striker's implement since time immemorial. G.B. Buckley condenses this evolution admirably in his *Historical Gleanings* manuscript, held at Lord's:

'Originally all bats were made in one piece: but the date when they were first made from a blade and a handle is not known. The sequence of events is probably as follows:– A one-piece bat with a broken handle was repaired by the insertion of a wooden handle into the blade. The repaired bat was found to be better than the original. Bats were then made from blades and wooden handles. This might have been in the 1830s. Then came the first "spring handled" bat, followed by the one with a single strip of whalebone in the handle, then that with three strips, and finally, about 1855, the cane handled bat.' Buckley was only a little late. It was in 1853 that a craftsman-cricketer named Thomas Nixon had conceived the idea of making the handle itself springy with cane. Nixon had an inventive mind, for in 1841 he had introduced cork knee pads and then in 1862 he took out a patent with John Lillywhite on a bowling machine called the Balista.

Another innovation was to cover the pitch at Lord's with tarpaulin in the wet summer of 1872; a heavy roller had been first used at the ground two years earlier and practice nets five years before that. The experiment was repeated that year at Prince's Ground, where Middlesex played matches. Prince's was situated in what is now mainly an exclusive residential area between Knightsbridge and the King's Road, Chelsea, at Lennox Gardens with Milner Street on one side, where there is now 'The Australian' public house, and Walton Street on the other.

Player's dress naturally reflected the conventions of each period. Between 1850 and 1880 club caps or 'half-bowlers' were the usual headgear, with striped, checked or spotted coloured shirts. The All-England XI paraded white shirts with pink spots and in the early 1860s Oxford and Cambridge adopted their respective hues of blue to cover manly young torsos. Uni-toned and multi-coloured blazers arrived about the same time, and shoes gave way to boots, either brown or white with brown straps.

Between 1880 and the turn of the century there were further changes. White shirts with semi or fully-starched fronts became the norm and ties were worn

Several sizes too big but nothing daunted.

(*Right*) Spy on 'Ranji', from *Vanity Fair*, 1897.

(*Below*) A cricketing hero to be found in *Georgie's Money-Box*, *c.* 1880. The illustrator is R. André.

less frequently, though the bow tie remained. The shirts were usually high-buttoned or singlet style, the former sometimes finished off with low turned-down collars. The sweaters that began to be donned seem to have been first advertised in 1886, though they were in use before that date.

At Scarborough, on a very cold day in 1884, C.I. 'Buns' Thornton, the mighty smiter, went on to bowl his fast 'grubs'. He obviously had it in mind to amuse the crowd. First he divested himself of a coat or two, then a large sweater which used to cling below his knees when running, yet another sweater – a light one this time – and finally two waistcoats, all of which he handed with grand gestures to the unfortunate umpire, who doubtless felt akin to a clothes-horse.

On another occasion Thornton was seen at Sittingbourne, dressed in a borrowed nightshirt and stalking wild duck. He seemed irresistably attracted by water. At Malton, in Yorkshire, one day he had his eye on a pond in a corner of the ground. The opposing captain, realizing that such a tempting target could not be ignored by an intuitive hitter like Thornton, placed a man on the far side ready for a catch. Sure enough, 'Buns' took the bait, lofted a drive high over the middle of the pond and the unwary fielder, with eyes only for the ball, fell right in.

Thornton, who disdained gloves and pads because he believed they cramped his movement, was no mere slogger. Contemporary reports were unanimous in that view when recounting a match against Merchant Taylors during which he managed to lose seven balls. In a way this glorious striker epitomized the personalities that dominated cricket from the late 1850s to the advent of World War I. All were men of worth and the legends sprang from their deeds, seen at first hand from boundary edge and relayed in honest detail in the press of

An English School pen, black ink and watercolour picture, heightened with white. The illustration has a dig at two lengthy royal innings.

The Hon. Ivo Bligh's team returned having won nine and lost three of the seventeen matches played. They defeated Murdoch's men 2–1 in the series, bringing home the Ashes in the newly constituted urn, though they lost the encounter with a side representing the full strength of the colonies by four wickets.

ENGLAND *v.* AUSTRALIA 1882-83
'THE TEST TEAM WHICH FIRST BROUGHT BACK THE ASHES'

| W. BARNES, | | F. MORLEY, | | C. T. STUDD, | | G. F. VERNON, | | O. F. H. LESLIE, |
| G. B. STUDD, | | E. F. S. TYLECOTE, | | THE HON. IVO BLIGH, | | A. G. STEEL, | | W. W. READ, |
| | | R. G. BARLOW, | | | | W. BATES, | | |

(*Next page left*) Embossed lithographically-printed paper images, popular during Victorian and Edwardian times and known colloquially as scraps, portrayed cricketers in many poses.

(*Next page right*) Postcard pot-pourri. Ripe for ridicule.

the day. They were fortunate in not having to contend with a reduction in stature through telefoto lens, cosy post-match interviews or libellous gossip.

Several of these personalities were to be found in the powerful Cambridgeshire side of the 1860s. 'Tear 'em' Tarrant, who could inject terrifying pace from around the wicket on the line of the batsmen's legs; two outstanding batsmen, Tom Hayward and Robert Carpenter, one a stylist, the other a 'fierce rapacious aggressor'; and gifted leg-spinner Billy Buttress, a most convincing ventriloquist who, when travelling on the railway, practised to remarkable effect his motley selection of untamed animals. Buttress was never in search of a seat.

Around the same time Richard Daft, of Nottinghamshire, a most fully equipped professional batsman, and his colleagues George Parr – he captained the first official tour to North America and the second to Australia – and the burly penetrative fast bowler 'Foghorn' Jackson, were helping to make the north midlanders a force to be feared.

As for the other counties, Yorkshire had George Freeman and Tom Emmett, Surrey had William Caffyn and Julius Caesar and Middlesex had the reputable Walker brotherhood of Southgate. They also had for one match the effervescent R.S. Fitzgerald, who had graduated by way of the Harrow XI, Cambridge Quidnuncs, MCC and I. Zingari. An attractive batsman and witty writer – *Jerks-in from Short-leg and Wickets in the West* are still much sought-after – he became the first paid secretary to the MCC. He twice led sides abroad, to Paris in 1867 and to the United States and Canada in 1872. A man of humour, with a flair for forward thinking, he took a surprisingly traditionalist view of a proposed

Making a good score.

charitable game at Lord's played by a band of Clown Cricketers in 1875. Fitzgerald felt that Clown Cricket was a burlesque not to be tolerated at headquarters. Whether he was right or not is debatable.

Farcical cricket with the Clowns, 1875.

The Clowns' antics on the cricket field could be said to have provided a kind of interval diversion between the era of the touring elevens and the consolidation of the county championship, though the three overlapped to a greater or lesser extent and, in any case, there are differing opinions as to when the county tourney first became operational. Some favour 1873, many more 1890 – and they are not the only dates.

The Clowns did, however, excite considerable interest for about ten years up to the late 1870s and there were a number of separate troupes going around the country. A typical match would involve the use of trick bats through which a ball would disappear and the turning of somersaults when a wicket fell or the umpire called 'Over'.

A cricketing gaslamp.

Several first-class cricketers appeared as Clowns under assumed names, among them W.R. Gilbert of Gloucestershire and David Eastwood, Tom Emmett and Edmund Peate of Yorkshire. Peate was a member of Treloar's troupe who, according to Haygarth, embarked on a tour of America in 1876, although there is no record of their doings 'over there' in libraries or from other likely sources.

Prominent Clown troupes included that of Harry Croueste; King and Casey's

A different stage for the players at the Scarborough Festival in 1885.

England v Australia, September 1880 at Kennington Oval.

(later Casey and Robson's); the Imperial Clown Cricketers and the London Clowns. The fun and the farce did not last though; a joke played often enough begins to pall.

Starting to make his considerable physical presence tell in no uncertain way was one W.G. Grace. Somehow Grace was and is Victorian England. It is impossible to separate him from the time or to think of him as purely a cricketer. A hundred years later he stands, in the mind's eye of many, as one of a quaternity representing an epoch, the others being Gladstone, Disraeli and Dickens. It is difficult now to think of W.G as just one of a seventy-strong family group (albeit an important one), many of whom put bat to ball. Mother Martha, shrewd enough to take her big son into the back garden at 'The Chestnuts', Downend, and teach him all the strokes he would need to confound the cricket world (or so we are told); Dr. Henry Mills Grace, who founded a club called 'The Mangotsfield', which beat all rivals in the neighbourhood and led to the formation of the West Gloucestershire CC; elder son Henry, a good all-rounder, who played for South Wales against the MCC at Lord's; second son Alfred, keen on many sports and an able cricketer; Edward Mills, 'E.M. – The Coroner', first of the famous three whose boisterous feats on the field were eclipsed only by those of the ubiquitous 'W.G.' and George Frederick, 'G.F.', a punishing batsman, fast round-arm bowler and magnificent fielder who brought off one of the most famous deep field catches in the history of the game. Then, of course, there were all the sisters, cousins, uncles, aunts, relatives-in-law, etcetera. Once there was even a game between Eleven Grace Girls and Eleven Grace Boys . . .

William Gilbert Grace started badly! His first public appearance with the bat brought a paltry four runs from four innings. Mind you, he was then only nine years of age. By his sixteenth year, and with the encouragement of an incipient beard, he had developed a technical mastery that produced 170 and 56 not out for South Wales versus The Gentlemen of Sussex. Eleven years after that, in 1875, and still only in his twenties, he stood alone on a pinnacle with more runs and more centuries than any other player in the history of the game.

Statistics can be burdensome to those who regard cricketing arithmetic as a trivial adjunct to the cumulative value of figures of character on the field of play. But Grace's phenomenal achievements breach that defensive wall by their sheer measure. In 1871 he accumulated 2,739 runs, the first time any player had reached 2,000 in a first-class season. In 1874 he became the first player

Even the weather must not be allowed to dismiss Dr. Grace.

The bat with which W.G. Grace scored 159 for Lord Sheffield's XI against Victoria at Melbourne in 1891.

(*Right*) 'Spelter' figure of Grace.

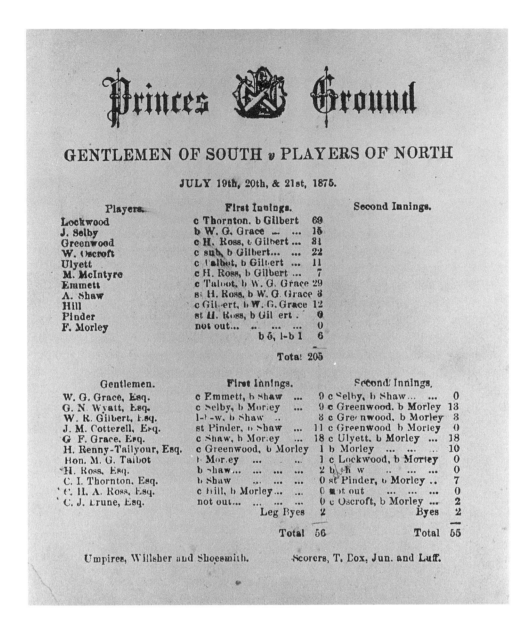

# Princes Ground

## GENTLEMEN OF SOUTH v PLAYERS OF NORTH

### JULY 19th, 20th, & 21st, 1875.

| Players. | First Innings. | | Second Innings. | |
|---|---|---|---|---|
| Lockwood | c Thornton. b Gilbert | 69 | | |
| J. Selby | b W. G. Grace ... ... | 15 | | |
| Greenwood | c H. Ross, b Gilbert ... | 31 | | |
| W. Oscroft | c sub. b Gilbert... ... | 22 | | |
| Ulyett | c Talbot, b Gilbert ... | 11 | | |
| M. McIntyre | c H. Ross, b Gilbert ... | 7 | | |
| Emmett | c Talbot, b W. G. Grace | 29 | | |
| A. Shaw | st H. Ross, b W. G. Grace | 3 | | |
| Hill | c Gilbert, b W. G. Grace | 12 | | |
| Pinder | st H. Ross, b Gilbert | 0 | | |
| F. Morley | not out ... ... ... | 0 | | |
| | b 5, l-b 1 | 6 | | |

**Total 205**

| Gentlemen. | First Innings. | | Second Innings. | |
|---|---|---|---|---|
| W. G. Grace, Esq. | c Emmett, b Shaw ... | 9 | c Selby, b Shaw... ... | 0 |
| G. N. Wyatt, Esq. | c Selby, b Morley ... | 9 | c Greenwood. b Morley | 13 |
| W. R. Gilbert, Esq. | l-b-w. b Shaw ... | 8 | c Greenwood b Morley | 3 |
| J. M. Cotterell, Esq. | st Pinder, b Shaw ... | 11 | c Greenwood b Morley | 0 |
| G. F. Grace, Esq. | c Shaw, b Morley ... | 18 | c Ulyett. b Morley ... | 18 |
| H. Renny-Tailyour, Esq. | c Greenwood, b Morley | 1 | b Morley ... ... ... | 10 |
| Hon. M. G. Talbot | b Morley ... ... ... | 1 | c Lockwood, b Morley | 0 |
| H. Ross, Esq. | b Shaw ... ... ... | 2 | b Shaw ... ... ... | 0 |
| C. I. Thornton. Esq. | b Shaw ... ... ... | 0 | st Pinder, b Morley .. | 7 |
| C. H. A. Ross, Esq. | c Hill, b Morley... ... | 0 | not out ... ... ... | 0 |
| C. J. Lrune, Esq. | not out... ... ... ... | 0 | c Oscroft, b Morley ... | 2 |
| | Leg Byes | 2 | Byes | 2 |
| | **Total 56** | | **Total 55** | |

Umpires, Willsher and Shoesmith.    Scorers, T. Box, Jun. and Luff.

Princes Ground housed many important games during the second half of the nineteenth century.

James Lillywhite Jnr., member of the famous family, who captained England in the first two Test Matches.

to perform the 'double' and two years later the first to score 2,000 runs and take 100 wickets in the one season. In 1876 also, he scored the first first-class triple century and a few days later the second. In all Grace achieved the 'double' seven times, took 100 wickets in a summer nine times, and collected a thousand runs in a season twenty-eight times. In 1895, when he was forty-six, he made 1,000 runs in May, the first to accomplish this exceptional feat. It was in this year too that he became the first to reach 100 first-class centuries, which inspired composer John Harcourt Smith to put together some celebratory verses with music, unsurprisingly entitled 'The Song of the Centuries'.

Grace captained England thirteen times in a Test career spanning twenty seasons – indeed he hit the first English Test hundred. He toured Australia twice and North America once and spent practically thirty years as captain of Gloucestershire before switching his allegiance to London County. His final first-class match was at the Oval in 1908, when he turned out for the Gentlemen of England against Surrey on a bitterly cold Easter Monday and the succeeding days. *Wisden's Almanack* reports that 'the famous veteran kept up his wicket for two hours on the Tuesday and played very well indeed in the follow-on'.

In his sixtieth year, Grace scored 15 and 25 and bowled twelve balls for 5 runs without taking a wicket.

Nobody can be certain that they have accounted for every single run, wicket or catch that this cricket colossus amassed in his lifetime, though two devotees of the great man and his deeds, G. Neville Weston and Maurice Alexander, have by assiduous research over many years reached as definitive a verdict as is ever likely with the *minor matches* in presenting the following staggering totals:

|  | Runs | Wickets | Catches | Stump-ings |
|---|---|---|---|---|
| In First-Class Matches: | 54,904 | 2,879 | 871 | 3 |
| In Minor Matches: | 45,283 | 4,578 | 656 | 52 |
| Grand Totals: | 100,187 | 7,457 | 1,527 | 55 |

In recent years, the Association of Cricket Statistics has done much sterling work in clarifying the muddle surrounding what is and what is not first-class. Members Philip Bailey and Derek Lodge are two of a great number who have offered sound reasons for revising the *first-class* match figures for Grace that had been accepted for many years. Their totals read:

| Runs | Wickets | Catches | Stumpings |
|---|---|---|---|
| 54,211 | 2808 | 874 | 5 |

Presumably, however, with some first-class reverting to minor, the overall figures should be much the same.

Legends attract myths and the Grace legend was no exception. Of apocrypha there was no need; the subject himself was the mostly unwitting source of a

Bushier than ever. A.J.W.T. Manuel caricature of the Great Man in black pen and ink, pencil and crayon.

C. J. Kortright.   J. R. Mason.   A. C. Maclaren.   J. A. Dixon,   West, Umpire.
S. M. J. Woods,   A. E. Stoddart.   W. G. Grace.   C. L. Townsend.   F. S. Jackson,
Captain Wynyard,        G. MacGregor.

Gentlemen v. Players
(Played at Lord's).

W. G. Grace's Jubilee, July 1898.

Photo by E. Hawkins and Co., Brighton.

IN A CORNISH PAVILION (*after* H. S. TUKE, R.A.).

The *Punch* Summer Number of 1922 showed studies in the manner of four distinguished Royal Academicians with cricket as a motif.

THE DEMON BATSMAN (*after* AUGUSTUS JOHN, A.R.A.).

COUNTRY HOUSE CRICKET (*after* C. SIMS, R.A.).

THE WILLOW-BEARER (*after* G. CLAUSEN, R.A.).

rich choice of anecdote. Stories about Grace could and do help fill books, and a selection can be no more than personal. Many revolve around his reluctance to accept lbw dismissals; he was known to regard lbw as an unsatisfactory and indeterminate way to finish an innings. In a game between Essex and Gloucestershire at Leyton in 1898 Grace clashed with the fiery fast bowler Charles Kortright. Kortright had already dismissed two batsmen for nought when he appealed for a glaringly obvious caught-and-bowled against W.G. Apparently a thunderous frown from the idol of the age persuaded the umpire to signal 'not out'. Kortright was not best pleased.

He was even less so later in the innings when further appeals for lbw and a catch behind the wicket were similarly rejected. Then Kortright fired in a totally unplayable delivery that uprooted the middle and leg stumps. With noticeable hesitation Grace began to leave the crease.

'Surely you're not going, Doc?' said the bowler, with mock surprise, 'There's still one stump standing.'

An equally involuntary dismissal, this time on the part of the fielder, occurred in the first match of R.A. Fitzgerland's 1872 North American tour against Montreal. Grace had scored 81 convincing runs, when he struck hard towards Mr. Benjamin, 'a stout fielder with spectacles on his nose and a pipe in his mouth, who suddenly received the ball in his abdomen, where it lodged and the Champion of England was forced to retire caught'.

It would be easy to exaggerate Grace's occasional unwillingness to accept an umpire's decision. Undoubtedly he realized and relished his star status as a Victorian hero with all its accompanying responsibilities. 'Admission charge 3d. If Dr. Grace plays 6d.' is a telling comment.

'The silver testimony of the turnstiles' produced tangible assets for Grace as well as for cricket. Technically an amateur, he regularly pocketed match fees of between £20–£36 a game throughout the 1880s and '90s to pay, he claimed, his *locum tenens* while he, Grace tended the public state of mind with healthy strokes to all parts.

More than once his medical knowledge was put to good use on the cricket field. An oft-recounted occasion was at Old Trafford in 1887. In attempting to stop a ball travelling over the boundary at the Stretford End, the Gloucestershire all-rounder, A.C.M Croome, impaled himself on the spiked railings, severely gashing his throat. Without doubt Croome's life was saved by the inimitable Doctor, who, unfatigued after recent lengthy fielding and bowling stints, held the jagged edges of the wound together in a vice-like grip with his huge hands perfectly still for nearly half-an-hour until needle and thread arrived to stitch the integument. In the general imagination this vividly real event followed an all-night accouchement, a breakfast of raw herrings and brandy and a train delayed so that Grace might get to the match on time. Such had been the impingement on Victorian consciousness of England's Hercules. He personified virtues they held most dear – courage, fortitude, self-denial and endurance, and his middle-class roots increased identification for the majority. Conan Doyle described Grace as '*un homme legendaire* in his own time'. When he died of a stroke in October 1915 the gloom of the Great War and the passing of what had been, for so many, the embodiment of the spirit of a Golden Age, caused unrelieved depression throughout the land.

Predominant though Grace had been until almost the turn of the century, he was not alone in cricket's hall of fame. Nottinghamshire had the illustrious opener, Arthur Shrewsbury, who in the 1880s twice led England to success

One of many great achievements by the Yorkshire and England all-rounder.

A Christie's catalogue description reads: *A brass-cased mantel timepiece, the case formed as a wicket and crossed bats, centred by a circular ivorine dial with Arabic numerals, on oval naturalistic Gash, raised on Gun fleet – $6\frac{1}{4}$ in. high.*

(*Next page left*) A notable patron of the game, the Earl of Sheffield, who gave his name to Australia's domestic competition, was renowned for sumptuous banquets with menu-cards to match.

(*Next page right*) Sitting aloofly. The autocratic Lord Hawke captured by 'Spy' (Leslie Ward) in Vanity Fair, 1892.

Gargoyle of Lord Harris.

Cricketing letterhead for a masonic lodge, *c.* 1910.

in Australia – Grace regarded him as 'the finest *professional* batsman of his day' – and also Alfred Shaw. Shaw was the most economical slow-medium bowler of his generation, delivering more overs than he conceded runs. A scheming master of line and length, he took 100 wickets in a season eight times, and had outstanding analyses both for and against MCC. In 1874 he dismissed all ten in an innings for 73 runs against the North, and a year later took seven of the club wickets at a nominal cost of 7 runs for his home county. Shaw captained England four times and at various periods coached, jointly promoted tours and partnered a sports goods firm with his colleague Shrewsbury.

There were many others whose very names are now redolent of the uncompromising certainties and quirkish stances of late Victorian and early Edwardian England. The Lancastrian pair Barlow and Hornby, of Francis Thompson's repining poem *At Lord's* (Thompson also wrote a comparison of the lissome virtuosity of the Indian Prince, Ranjitsinghi, with that of the old masters); the Surrey stalwarts Walter Read, George Lohmann and Bobby Abel; Yorkshire's Peel and Ulyett; and the brilliant all-round athlete, often likened to a Greek god, A.E. Stoddart, who played for both Middlesex and England at cricket and rugby and who tragically took his own life when the cavernous despondency of solitude replaced the cascading cheers of an admiring crowd.

Those noble lords Harris and Hawke, autocrats in their respective southern and northern fiefdoms, Kent and Yorkshire, and also wielding great power at headquarters, were from a line of venerable oaks that nowadays tends to get chipped at by some who carry theirs (chips, that is) on both shoulders. Doubtless this formidable duo at various times pronounced views and initiated actions

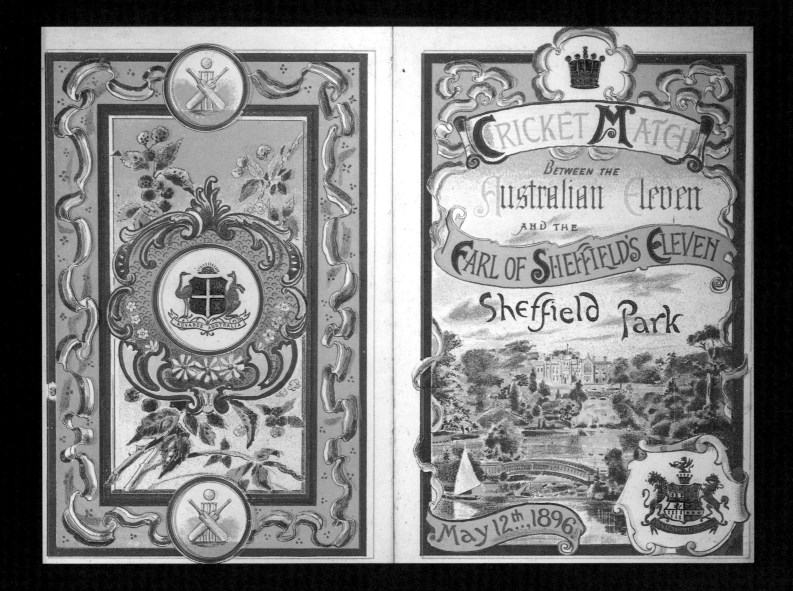

CRICKET MATCH
BETWEEN THE
Australian Eleven
AND THE
EARL OF SHEFFIELD'S ELEVEN
Sheffield Park

ADVANCE AUSTRALIA

May 12th., 1896.

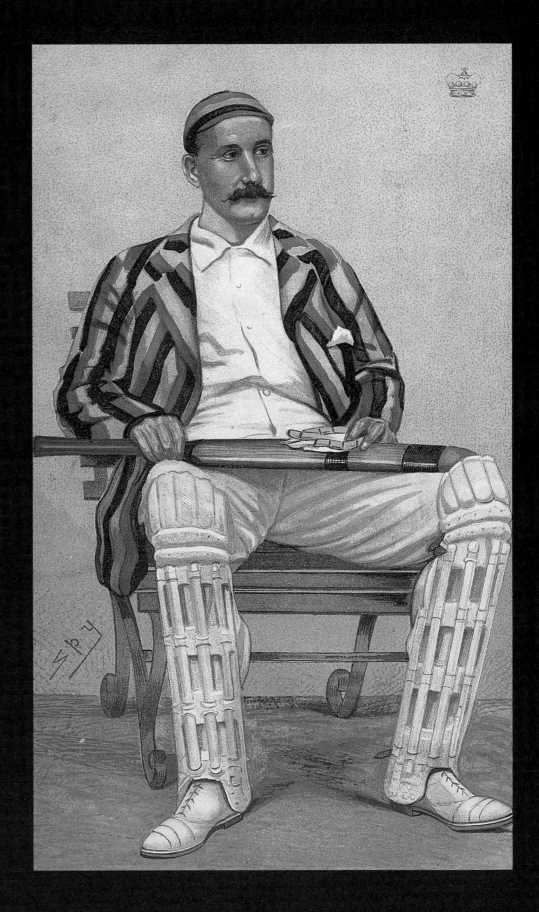

Reproduction nineteenth-century brolly stand from the Burlington Gallery.

(*Right*) A page from a scrapbook.

(*Next page*) Obstructing the fielder. Eton v Harrow, circa 1870s.

Bookplate used by Desmond Eagar (Hampshire County Cricket Club).

that to the late twentieth-century liberally-minded seem little short of tyrannical, yet always their motivation had been the essential good of the game. Harris, who once said 'My whole life is pivoted on Lord's', was a man of unimpeachable fairness if a certain rigidity. For him the laws of cricket were sacrosanct: 'Rules,' he remarked, 'are made to be broken, laws are made to be kept.' He forfeited Kent's return match with Lancashire in 1885 as a protest against the bowling of Nash and Crossland who, it was generally felt, 'threw' the ball. Harris captained England and held high office at Lord's and in public life, including the posts of Under-Secretary for India and Governor of Bombay.

Bowly's Back Play

Phillips a-rinting

Jack Lilly

Long-Tom.

Hawke was another staunch supporter of the professional cricketer, though an exacting martinet when it came to standards of behaviour. An old Etonian like Harris, he too captained England and adopted a draconian approach to most matters of moment. He deserves great credit, though, for instituting winter pay and trying to give financial stability to those who did not have any.

Throughout this first Golden Age other Etonians, old and new, were busily parading more immediate skills at Lord's, as they had been ever since a lame Byron had managed a total of nine runs for Harrow – batting in partnership for some of the time with a boy called Shakespear – when the annual encounter first took place on the famous ground in 1805. Already episodes from matches of the privileged triune, Eton, Harrow and Winchester, had assumed folkloric proportions: Dr. Heath's flogging of the entire Eton XI for defying his order not to play Westminster – no doubt the recipients felt there was nothing mythical about this; Beau Brummell, described by Gronow as the 'best scholar, the best boatman and the best cricketer' during his time at the school, and John Keate, who had distinguished himself in the XI and later returned as headmaster, a stern disciplinarian who ruled over the 'snobbiest democracy of the age'.

Broadcaster and priest, Cormac Rigby, in an illuminating Oxford PhD thesis, has counted among Keate's pupils 'sixteen dukes, fifteen marquesses, more than fifty earls and countless lesser nobility' and comments that 'this cream of the nobly-born encouraged a steady stream of the nearly-noble to follow them'. Despite dispensing harsh treatment Dr. Keate retained the affection of his flock with his love of cricket, and would frequently call the register on the playing fields to save the assembly having to change and return to the school buildings. Rigby recounts that 'in retirement Keate was once found with his coat off, surrounded by a parcel of children, playing cricket, and the first words heard by an approaching visitor were "Mrs. Keate, that's not fair – petticoat before wicket".'

An early colourful delineation of Eton cricket is to be found on a fish-strainer once owned by historian Philip Norman; another perhaps less bizarre location for reflection on the public school and their rivals is in a humorous, Latin skit *In Memoriam gloriosam ludorum* by Frederick Gale, and many jests at the expense of the Harvey-Bathursts, Bromley-Davenports, Knatchbull-Hugessons, Ruggles-Brises and their chinless chums, lounging with bright young things over the Fortnum and Mason hampers, are to be found in the pages of Punch.

The Gentlemen and Players' contests had started at Lord's in 1806, one year after Eton and Harrow had first ventured onto Dorset Square. Thirteen years were to pass before the engagement was renewed and over the next near century and a half the Players came out on top more often than not. As Victoria declined and a new era loomed the encounter was generally the classic of the English season, such players as Grace, Briggs, Jackson and Fry often having a decisive impact on the outcome. The Lord's game was sometimes augmented by forays to Brighton, Hastings, Folkestone, the Oval, Scarborough and elsewhere. Geoffrey Moorhouse sums up the meetings thus: 'Apart from anything else, the fixture exhibited the specifically amateur ingredient of cricket, a lightness that professionalism can rarely afford to the same degree. A certain amount of humbug went with it at times, latterly identified as "shamateurism", and Gents v Players by definition always embodied a number of caste marks that had become progressively unacceptable to the nation at large. None the less the genuine amateur gifts to the game have been sorely missed since the genuine amateur disappeared.' The last match took place in 1962.

Another anachronism, in the view of some non-traditionalists, is the continued mounting at Lord's of the annual Oxbridge encounter. Many argue for first-class status to be withdrawn, since academic policy at both universities makes it virtually impossible for anybody who can offer sporting prowess but little else – a chance to display it. Long gone are the less exacting regimes at Oxford and Cambridge when, supposedly, a distinguished cricketer, unable to answer the examination questions, instead wrote a pithy expletive across his paper. His tutor sadly remarked that he would have passed him for that one word if only he had spelt it correctly. Radicals of today advance the claims of such seats of learning as Durham and Manchester, and make a strong case for a Combined Universities side to take part in the two-innings games against the counties. Such a combination performs creditably in the Benson and Hedges Cup Competition.

As the years pass distance adds enchantment to the days of yore, when 'Old Stump' – Abel Kidd – was producing his quaint odes to the Light and Dark blues. The historical tablets recall an early captain of Cambridge, Arthur Wood, son of William, the saviour of Lord's, whose weight fluctuated between 20 and 28 stone and who spent much of his time updoing and undoing the 38 buttons on his waistcoat. Etched also are the vintage elevens: the 1890 Cambridge side led by Australian Sammy Woods, containing D.L.A. Jephson, F.S. Jackson, C.P. Foley, F.G.J. Ford and G. MacGregor; the 1900 Oxford team captained by R.E. Foster and including J.W.F. Crawford, H. Martyn, C.H.B. Marsham, B.J.T. Bosanquet and innumerable others whose names became part of the panoply of late nineteenth-century to mid-twentieth century cricket, when a flowering talent revealed Peter May, Colin Cowdrey, David Sheppard, Hubert Doggart, Raman Subba Row, Clive Van Ryneveld and M.J.K. Smith. A resumé of the eminent players who have graced Fenners and Parks over the years would take a book in itself and is inextricable from the leadership of the game in practically every avenue.

These terse tracings of three institutions within cricket's time should not prevent our return to a stray line of thought on matters significant from around a hundred years ago. By then there were special telegraph installations at seven major grounds – Bramall Lane, Derby, Old Trafford, Park Avenue, Trent Bridge, Lord's and the Oval – to relay the events of the day, and it was estimated that the 10 o'clock editions of the London evening papers sold some 25,000 copies purely on the strength of the scores within. Sydney Pardon had founded a cricket reporting agency; Wisden finally outgunned all the Lillywhites, the colour of James's Annual reflecting the message at the bank, so that it gave best to the Almanack in 1900; separate business concerns such as Wright and Co. and Maurice and Co. issued catalogues of cricket books for purchase as did individual dealers like Alfred Gaston and John Rob; two bibliographies were printed in eleven years and the magazine *Cricket* spanned three decades.

The gentry was finding country house cricket to its liking. The languid action at Broughton-Gifford games and Backwell Robinson family matches is preserved for posterity in scorebooks embroidered with the remnants of chocolate cake and spilled tea. Some most gentle and *parfait* knights, notably Frank Benson, James Barrie and John Squire, ran theatrical and literary elevens renowned for laughable lunges and bungled bowling. Nevertheless the Allahakbarries and Invalids lost nothing in team title to club outfits more ably equipped such as the Incapables, Ishmaelites, Yellowhammers and Devon Dumplings.

A League was instituted by the Gas, Light and Coke Co. but they had to

The Original English Lady Cricketers comprised a troupe of two professional teams organized to tour the country. The exhibition games were stage-managed to a large extent and soon lost their initial appeal. Apparently, it was said at the time that they might be original and English, but they were neither ladies nor cricketers!

(*Next page left*) 'She shot one glance at Hilda' R.H. Brock's illustration of cricket with the fairer sex in *Delightful Stories for Girls*, *c*. 1929.

(*Next page right*) A heady mixture.

Edwardian ladies' team and mascot, gathered together in all their finery for possibly a fun game.

wait some thirty years before the Electric Light Cricket Council shed some sunshine with the issue of a book of rules. Banks and breweries formed teams for their employees, Lord's overcame threats from the advancing railway, there had been a strike for more pay at an Oval Test match and the follow-on became optional.

The game was everywhere. References to its terms were incorporated into constitution and conversation. 'That's not cricket' headed a Suffragette handbill protesting the denial of the franchise to women who paid taxes – a distinct advance from a few years earlier, when the firm of Gamages had been instructed to produce a *blue* cricket ball for use at ladies matches in case the fair sex should swoon at the sight of a rubicund projectile. And this was even more pronounced autonomy from the team of 1890 professional 'Original English Lady Cricketers', who travelled the country accompanied by a chaperone, playing exhibition matches under assumed names.

Edwardian cricket was progressive, secure in the knowledge that it held the attention of the majority who relished summer sporting entertainment. 'There was sufficient leisure to provide an abundance of amateurs, while the life of the modestly successful professional was prosperous and agreeable compared to the lot of the working man' writes Ian Peebles. Maybe so, though generalizations about living standards should be treated with care. There is no doubt,

The drink of the "Century"
DEWAR'S
# "White Label"
THE *RIGHT* LABEL

Gently perspiring. A Fan, made by Eugene Rimmfell, that was presented to lady spectators at the Eton v Harrow encounter at Lord's, 1876.

(*Left*) Cricket used as a political *Punch* by Linley Sambourne in 1892.

*'On the bat's back I do fly*
*After the Ashes merrily.'*
    (cf. *The Tempest*, Act V, Scene 1)
Cartoonist Bernard Partridge's welcoming *Punch* to the Australian Cricket Team, 1905.

however, about his assertion that 'English county cricket was as at its zenith in the years preceding the First World War. There was still some foundation for the saying that love of county was greater than love of country. The levelling, centralizing effects of broadcasting and the mass-produced motor car were still far away, and to the ordinary citizen the borders of his county were very real. Where cricket was concerned the setting had all the attractions of the 1890s but the game had developed in itself and expanded. The Championship was dominated during this time by Yorkshire, who won it no less than six times, and by Kent who, with four wins, ran them close. Middlesex, Lancashire, Nottinghamshire, Warwickshire and Surrey shared what honours were left, which was a fair reflection of the balance of power.'

The County Championship had recruited all its present membership, with the exception of Glamorgan, when Northamptonshire were admitted in 1905. Jessop, MacLaren, Fry, Hirst and Rhodes put their skills on display, Hobbs, Hayward, Blythe and Spooner were making their mark and Sydney Barnes was proving himself a destructive opponent. The elegant Lionel Palairet, the ever-present Fosters and the rampaging Gunns added lustre to an already vividly colourful scene. Heroes from abroad came and went; the international exchange, with 'Plum' Warner to the fore, allowed a discerning public to appreciate the talents of Australia's finest, Trumper, Jackson, Hill and Noble, and South Africa's best, the sensational spin quartet of Vogler, Faulkner, Schwartz and White. Bosanquet discovered the 'googly' and as a new craft arrived an old one disappeared. G.H. Simpson-Hayward, of Worcestershire, who took over 400 wickets in this first Golden Age, was one of the 'last of the lobsters'.

This happy *tableau* was fractured by conflict, with the first World War taking a dreadful toll. An incomplete list of victims in the 1920 Wisden numbered 77, and that consisted of relatively well-known players including the forceful Kenneth Hutchings, Colin Blythe, the master of left-arm deceptive flight, a potential England fast bowler Percy Jeeves – before Wodehouse – and the young A.E.J. Collins, who had made the highest individual score in any form of organized cricket. The Australian fast bowler 'Tibby' Cotter was also killed in action. In *Pageant of Cricket*, David Frith records that Cotter had a premonition of his imminent death. Before being felled at Beersheba, 'he tossed up a ball of mud and said to a mate: "That's my last bowl, Blue. Something's going to happen."'

This stark vignette recalls the Boer hostilities a generation earlier, when Captain Valentine Dodd, in the act of bowling, was struck down by an errant shell. Not all premature passings were attributable to war though; the tragic loss through Bright's disease of the unsurpassable Victor Trumper was universally mourned.

After the cataclysm it was difficult to pick up the pieces. Social attitudes had changed and revolutionary ideas had percolated through to the cricket field. Most of the notions were not implemented. A preposterous suggestion to dispense with left-handers was laughed out of court, and a less absurd move to penalize the batting side when a maiden over was bowled was firmly resisted. The scheme for two-day county cricket was tried in 1919, but the preponderance of drawn games brought a rapid resumption of the normal three-day outing the next year. The standard of English cricket was suffering through lack of practice, and it took the glorious summer of 1921 to nurse it along the road to recovery.

All lovers of cricket cherish their own summers of complete contentment,

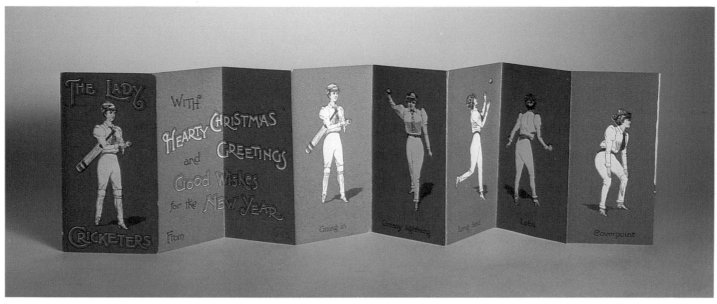

(*Above*) A Victorian card in eight folding sections each with different cricketing captions.

(*Right*) A water-jug picturing the 'unbowlable' Australian captain and opening batsman, W.M. Woodfull. 1930.

(*Left*) Answer: 'No, I'm a ferrct, I go after the rabbits.' A pen, black ink and water-colour drawing by James Thorpe, which appeared in *The Tatler*, No. 625.

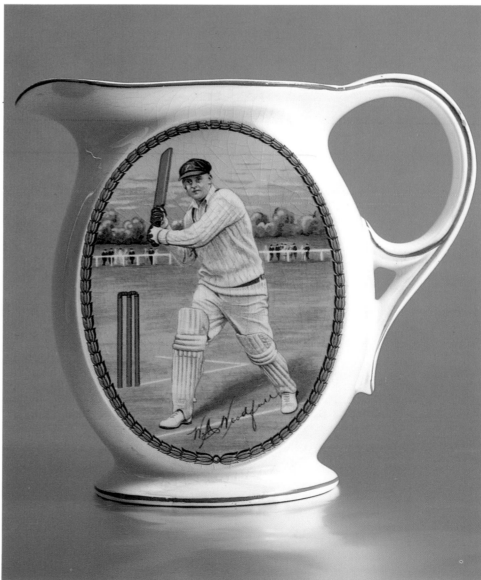

Tom Webster's cartoon from a 1930 *Daily Mail* prior to the Old Trafford Test.

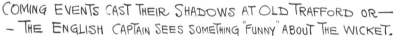

COMING EVENTS CAST THEIR SHADOWS AT OLD TRAFFORD OR—
— THE ENGLISH CAPTAIN SEES SOMETHING "FUNNY" ABOUT THE WICKET.

when the sky was never cloudy and the grass never blown, those lazy, hazy, crazy days of comfortable inertia, watching classic strokes and breathtaking bowling, the only dissenting voice that of deckchairs creaking under the transferred weight from now-empty picnic baskets. Yet if we reluctantly allow our private Arcadian settings to recede and seek a public consensus for cricket's second *Saturnia regna* a large show of hands would support the thriving twenties and throbbing thirties.

Conscious of Charles Caleb Colton's truism 'how strange it is that we of the present day are constantly praising that past age which our fathers abused, and as constantly abusing that present age, which our children will praise' it is nevertheless indisputable that those two decades were piping times for cricket. Once again, after an interregnum, some old conquerors remained and some new ones arrived. After a bout of ill-health Hobbs continued in masterly fashion. Partnered by Sandham for Surrey and Sutcliffe for England, he was perhaps the finest batsman of all time. The incomparable man of Kent, Frank Woolley, whose elegant batting overshadows a very real claim as the greatest all-rounder – who can match nearly 59,000 first-class runs, over 2,000 wickets and more than 1,000 catches? – delighted crowds wherever he played. 'Patsy' Hendren, Middlesex's energetic run-scorer, who accumulated 170 centuries, second only to Hobbs in the major listings, and hit no fewer than four double centuries on the 1929–30 West Indies tour, never seemed off-form throughout his career. Wally Hammond, whose batting veered from breathtaking brilliance to statuesque nobility, 'statistically dominated County cricket during the 1930s and headed the first-class batting averages for eight successive summers'. 'Tich' Freeman bamboozled 3,776 batsmen into involuntarily giving up their wickets (some of that number were the same individuals, of course, who could never quite fathom the leg-break from the top-spinner) and took 100 wickets in a

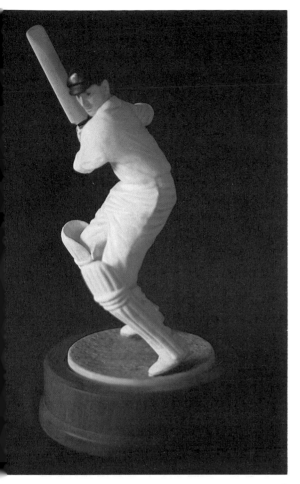

(*Above*) Jack Hobbs. One of a series of old English bone china figures depicting the game's great players, and sculpted by Count André D'Aquino.

(*Below*) A present from 'The Master' whilst playing for Vizianagram's team in India and, as it was then, Ceylon:
*To my dear friend, the Maharaj Kumar of Vizianagram. JB Hobbs. 21st December 1930.*
*I used this bat in my last Test Match v Australia at the Oval, August 1930. Also while scoring my first century in India at Benares, November, 1930 – – – – – JB Hobbs.*

season seventeen times, 200 eight times and 300 once. Then there were Freeman's Kentish colleague, Leslie Ames, of 'the dark eye and colouring of Romany blood', a batsman/wicket-keeper on the highest plane; the excitingly unpredictable Hampshire all-rounder George Brown, of striking Red Indian appearance; his obdurate run-machine team-mate Philip Mead; the indiosyncratic Surrey captain, Percy Fender, who scored the fastest century in first-class cricket; the stubborn, unyielding 'Johnny' Douglas of Essex, who had won an Olympic Gold at boxing and an amateur international cap at soccer and who was drowned trying to save his father when the ship on which they were passengers was in collision in thick fog off the island of Laeso, Denmark; Maurice Tate, 'Percy' Chapman, Charlie Parker, Ken Farnes, Douglas Jardine, 'Gubby' Allen, Harold Larwood, Bill Voce, Bill Bowes, Jim Parks snr., Duleepsinhji, nephew of 'Ranji'; the Langridges – so many so good that one could go on and on. Nor should we forget the mighty Australians, Macartney, McDonald, Mailey, Gregory, Ponsford, Woodfull and, of course, Bradman; the West Indians, Constantine, Martindale and Headley and the prime personalities from South Africa, India and New Zealand.

These were eventful years. Radio commentary of cricket had been heard in Australia and then in England, and the Rev. F.R. Gillingham will forever be remembered for giving details of advertisements round the ground when rain stopped play, bringing down Reithian wrath from heaven, or rather the BBC. Jack Hobbs equalled, then beat, W.G. Grace's record of 126 first-class centuries and went on to a generally accepted 197; the lbw law was amended; the ball was reduced in circumference to between $8\frac{13}{16}$ inches and 9 inches – officially, although the dimensions had been prevalent for some years. Eight-ball overs were in force in Australia and ten-ball overs in Philadelphia; New Zealand could not make up its mind and played ducks and drakes between six and eight. The 'bodyline' controversy soured and nearly sundered relations between the two 'old enemies'. Staggering new records with bat and ball were made in various parts of the globe, and Bradman seemed to be the maker of every other one. Tours between established cricket-playing countries and those where the game was not so predominant increased enormously. A 'Timeless' Test was played in South Africa, Len Hutton made 364, a new world record for an innings in a Test Match, and a sixteen-year-old boy called Sheriff, from Melbourne, scored 1,004 runs in seven innings in a season without once being dismissed.

A cumulus coloured black was gathering over Europe and again it was time for cricketers everywhere to take off their whites and don khaki, navy and now blue. Again, without realizing it, some revered cricketers had scored their last run and taken their last wicket. Again the game would continue against the odds.

A match in progress at Hyde Park,
Sydney, *c.* 1842.

# The Spread Worldwide

Our journey so far, though sometimes circuitous, has remained largely on English soil. It is time now for fleeting visits to other parts to see how, throughout the nineteenth century and even earlier, disciples of the cricketing gospel had fingered every page of the atlas. Fundamentally, of course, the missionary work had been hand-in-glove with British imperialist rule, notwithstanding some practitioners pitching stumps in such unlikely venues as the Spitzbergen ice-cap and a bridge over the Bosphorus. An article in a *Blackwood's Edinburgh Magazine* of 1892 conveys the mood graphically: 'The Englishman carries his cricket bat with him as naturally as his gun case or his india rubber bath'. Even so, as we shall see, it was not only expat John Bulls who were aiming shooters at a wet patch from twenty-two yards.

As in much history, nobody can be sure of the exact dates when the game was first played in different parts of the world; all that can be said with certainty is that by such and such a time cricket was known to have made an appearance somewhere. Thus the naval chaplain, Henry Teonge, who kept a diary of his service aboard His Majesty's ships *Assistance*, *Bristol* and *Royal Oak* between 1675 and 1679, and noted English residents disporting themselves at several pastimes, including 'krickett', at a riverside haunt four miles outside Aleppo, secures a niche in the Bradshaw of bat versus ball and a singular mark for the Middle East.

The Navy and Army were catalysts for many early encounters. Seamen of the East India Company were playing cricket at Cambay, India, in 1721 and the military at Bombay in 1797. In the same year cricket was recorded at Seringapatum after the siege. Half a world away the Dublin Garrison had defeated All-Ireland by an innings in 1792 and fifty years before that a game at Munster had been described in an 'Irish gimblet'. The crews of His Majesty's ships had played cricket at Lisbon in 1736. As historian Rowland Bowen has pointed out, 'recreation had to be found for troops and sailors: cricket was an ideal source of it, and the very activity it demanded must often have been welcome to shipboard mariners'.

Throughout the 1700s there were periodic sightings of cricket in North America, though whether in every case the format followed the practice prevalent in the 'old country' is doubtful. The game enjoyed by one-time member of the Middle Temple William Byrd and his buddies, who rose at 6 am to play cricket beside the James river, in Virginia, was almost certainly an adap-

An Australian navy-blue velvet and gold braid appearance cap, named within Alfred Barrett, MH and H.

Cricket at Dagona, Papua New Guinea,
1968.

(*Right*) A Parisian's idea of 'ze mad Engleesh pastime'. A Draner lithograph of the front line.

(*Below*) Emigré lace-workers from Nottingham threading ties with the Paris Cricket Club in post-Napoleonic days at the Bois de Boulogne. Edmond Morin's depiction reveals the Englishmen's favourite drink.

LE JEU DE CRICKET. — Grand match disputé au bois de Boulogne entre les joueurs français et anglais. (Dessin de M. Edmond Morin. — (Voir les détails dans le *Courrier de Paris*.)

tation. A 'long low wicket' was in use for much cricket commenced by the colonists, however a match in New York in 1751 between the home side and a London XI was played according to 'the London method' – in other words, according to the code agreed in 1744. Maryland, Connecticut and Boston, New England, were among other states and centres that supported cricketing ventures, and recently-settled Highland Scots celebrated St. Andrew's Day by playing at Savannah, Georgia. Some idea of the perception of cricket in America after Independence can be gauged from a debate in the Constitutional Convention in Boston in 1790, during which an objection was taken to calling the Chief Executive of the United States of America a 'President' since a cricket club had a president.

Five years earlier, and two hundred or so miles north-west of the principal city of Massachusetts, French Canadians were playing cricket in Montreal, a reminder that in France itself the game had a footing. In 1766, Horace Walpole had watched cricket at Neuilly-sur-Seine, near Paris, and twelve years later Boydell issued an engraving depicting a match at Belle Isle. The aborted 1789 visit to the Bois de Boulogne, Paris, by a team of English cricketers under the Earl of Tankerville is another instance of an intended presence. The disorderly street situation surrounding the French Revolution and conflicting inflammatory rumours concerning British involvement hastened the Duke of Dorset's departure from his post as Ambassador to the Court of Versailles. Leaving behind the perilously-situated Marie Antoinette – his only close friend in France – the Duke arrived back in Dover just as the cricket team – sent by the Foreign Secretary, the Duke of Leeds, as a conciliatory goodwill gesture – were about to board the passage boat. Result, no tour, many retrospective what-might-have-beens and for the unaffected Duke a gradual retreat from the life he had enjoyed – the riches lavished on entertainment and cricket, his diamonds, his ornate scarf-pin, his Chinese page Hwang-a-Tung, his Italian mistress, Giannetta Baccelli, 'who caused so much scandal by dancing at the Opera in Paris with his Garter bound about her forehead' – to one of reclusion and a looming hereditary insanity.

After the Napoleonic Wars, and due extensively to the influx of lace-workers from Nottingham, cricket clubs were established at Dieppe, Boulogne, Calais, Bordeaux, St. Servan, St. Omer, Paris and, later, Arras, and there have been so-called 'international engagements' with Continental neighbours, as well as tours by representative sides from this country. At the 1900 Olympic Games in Paris the Devon County Wanderers represented Britain and beat the Athletic Club of Paris, representing France, by 158 runs at the Vélodrome de Vincennes – the only time cricket has been a part of that sporting jamboree. In 1987 a celebratory return match took place at Meudon.

It may be thought that the mainland of Europe has been an arid desert for cricket. This assumption would be only marginally true, for while the game has a distinctive countenance in Holland and Denmark its existence elsewhere has been transitory or very low-key. In *Punch*, in 1851, a waggish rationale surfaced: 'The game is essentially English and though our countrymen carry it abroad wherever they go, it is difficult to inoculate or knock it into the foreigner. The Italians are too fat for cricket; the French too thin; the Dutch too dumpy; the Belgians too bilious; the Flemish too flatulent; the East Indians too peppery; the Laplanders too bow-legged; the Swiss too sentimental; the Greeks too lazy; the Egyptians too long in the neck and the Germans too short in the wind.'

How to destroy the precepts of Dale Carnegie in a single paragraph, and how that critic would have been amused to learn that in recent years we have been blessed with two books that appertain: *The Story of Continental Cricket*, by Labouchere, Provis and Hargreaves, and *German Cricket*, a short history by Coldham.

A few other European excursions deserve noting. Cricket was played at Spa, in what were then the Austrian Netherlands, in 1768 and obviously in Rome in the 1790s, to judge from the well-known Sablet painting of furniture designer Thomas Hope in which he is taking a somewhat ungainly stance in front of a tiny wicket, while behind the stumps an interested onlooker holds a cloak in readiness for a wayward ball. Further south Colonel Francis Maceroni, aide-de-camp to Joachim Murat, King of Naples, formed a cricket club in the city in 1811 during the occupation with many French and Neapolitan officers as members. And, lo and behold, in recent years an Italian Cricket Association was formed and an uninhibited band of Mediterranean cricketers arrived in the UK for a tour.

In 1796 a book was published in Hamburg giving a detailed description of cricket, then five and six years later went into two Danish editions which lost a little accuracy in the translation. We read that 'the player "A" bowls the ball along the ground at speed to hit the rear wicket. Here the player "B" stands

Sartorial differences as seen in France around 1910.

An artistic impression by Joe Scarborough of Douglas Jardine acknowledging the plaudits at Bramall Lane, Sheffield. A very different reaction to the reception he received in Australia during the infamous 'Bodyline' Tour.

(*Below*) The umpire who confessed he wasn't looking!

ready to grasp the ball and bowl it in the same manner at the front wicket. The ball is thus bowled continuously from one wicket to the other.' Who said cricket was a slow game?

In Denmark and the Netherlands, who play one another regularly, the standard of the national teams has been good enough to defeat MCC and Australian sides. Danish cricket dates from the 1860s – at least the officially recorded matches do – when there were encounters between Copenhagen and Sorø Academy teams and a match at Randers, in Jutland. The Morild family, through several generations, have made an enormous contribution to the welfare of the game and latterly Ole Mortensen has been a striking force as an opening bowler, not only for Denmark but for Derbyshire in the county competitions. The Netherlands can boast a cricket club in Utrecht in 1855, formed by University men, though the oldest existing club, *Koninklijke Utile Dulci*, in Deventer, was founded twenty years later. There were eighteen clubs in the 1880s and by 1891 two competitive leagues. The following year a Dutch side, The Gentlemen of Holland, toured England. The cities of Amsterdam, Rotterdam, The Hague and Haarlem (with the famous *Rood en Wit* club) are the homes of most Dutch cricket. A player such as C.J. Posthuma, whom Grace rated highly enough to allow him to turn out for London County, and in the last couple of seasons Paul-Jan Bakker, who performs for Hampshire, help to emphasize how close the Netherlands have been, and indeed are, to breaking into top international company. They performed extremely creditably in the last ICC tourney and are hosting the next. Maybe the proximity of so many cricketers from around the world will provide just the inspiration needed to bridge the gap.

To expand on cricket's connection with each individual country in Europe would unbalance the game's importance at other more relevant points of the compass; suffice nods towards Germany, where there have been clubs at Berlin, Carlsruhe, Frankfurt, Cologne and other cities and towns; Switzerland with cricket at Geneva, Zuoz College, in the Engadine Valley, and, if writer Andrew Lang is to be believed, the market-place of Zug, where, with a camp-stool for a wicket, the confrontation 'came to a sudden termination owing to a tremendous slog over the bowler's head going through the Burgomaster's window'; Portugal, with clubs at Oporto and Lisbon, and a number of visits from distinguished sides including those of T. Westray and Sir Henry Leveson-Gower; Finland, where, during the 1980s, an enterprising band produced *The Helsinki Cricketer* magazine; and strangely not least, the Soviet Union.

Before the 1917 Revolution the land of the Czars contained two clubs for certain, possibly more, the St. Petersburg and the Alexandrossky, but the grounds were so rough and uneven that extras usually exceeded individual scores. Apparently Nicholas II liked cricket and actually had a cricket pitch prepared in the grounds of the Imperial Palace at Peterhof. Perhaps his interest sprang from being told of the occasion when Nicholas I attended a match on Chatham Lines and having watched for a few minutes, remarked: 'I don't wonder at the courage of you English when you teach your children to play with cannon-balls'. Not long ago, in a bookshop in Helsinki, a booklet of some fifty pages with a dozen illustrations was discovered. It contained a concise history of cricket and an account of its laws. Simply entitled *Cricket, the English Ball Game*, the work was written by M. Volkov in the pre-revolutionary alphabet and published by M.O. Volf, of Petrograd and Moscow, in 1915, not exactly the most propitious time to maximize sales. Such a venture surely denotes a wider interest in cricket in the region at that time than has been realized. In

This copper/zinc buckle could be the oldest known artefact depicting cricket outside the British Isles. Discovered by Clive Williams on the banks of the River Tweed in 1979, who has spent countless hours researching its origins. After much expert advice and delving in all sorts of fields, the owner puts forward the following theory: *that the buckle showing a young muscular slave mulatto being spectacularly bowled could have been commissioned by or for Commodore William Hotham, whose family had links with cricket of the time and also the Tweed Valley. Hotham was stationed in Barbados 1779/80 and the buckle would appear to be of that period.*

(*Next page left*) Intent spectators at Kolhapur, Maharashtra, India, November 1983. The match in progress between West Zone and West Indies resulted in a draw. The city was playing host to a touring team for the first time.

(*Next page right*) Stumps can be pitched anywhere. A street game in Karachi, Pakistan.

The Fourth Test Match of the 1901–02 tour at Sydney cricket ground. Having scored 317 in the first innings, with MacLaren making 92, England were bowled out by Saunders and Noble for 99 in their second knock and lost by 7 wickets.

most cricketing activity around Europe – though obviously British-inspired and centred on a nucleus of such as embassy staff, those on duties for the Crown, businessmen working abroad and voluntary exiles – there has been involvement in varying degrees by the local nationals.

Let us return to the mainstream development in the Commonwealth. The first recorded instances of cricket being played in Australia, South Africa and the West Indies fall within just five years from 1803 to 1808. *The Sydney Gazette and New South Wales Advertiser*, eight days into 1804, reports on 'the amateurs of cricket who scarce have lost a day for the past month' on Phillip's Common. *The Cape Town Gazette and African Advertiser* announces that 'a grand match at cricket will be played for 1,000 dollars a side on Tuesday, January 5th, 1808, between the officers of the artillery mess, having Colonel Austen of the 60th Regiment, and the officers of the Colony with General Clavering. The wickets are to be pitched at 10 o'clock.' And in Barbados we learn of a meeting of the St. Anne's Cricket Club in 1806. In both South Africa and the West Indies without doubt cricket was played at an earlier time. There is a tradition that during the first occupation of the Cape from 1795 to 1802, the garrison troops relieved their boredom with a game that reminded them of home. As far as the West Indies are concerned, the recovery in 1979 of a belt buckle showing a mulatto being bowled, points to mid-to-advanced eighteenth-century participation.

Australian cricket quickly developed an individual character and *Yorshire Post* cricket correspondent J.M. Kilburn put it memorably: It 'is a variation of the English game. The essentials are common but the details are different. Australian cricketers could not take over "the meadow game with the beautiful name" in precisely its English form because their meadows are not precisely as English meadows. Evening light and agricultural background based on the village community are not Australian characteristics encouraging sport. Facilities for Australian cricket have had to be created in the small township as in the big city and every step in the game's progress has had to be taken deliberately, with inevitable dispute over the appropriate way ahead.

'Survival demanded organization in Australian cricket. To play cricket at all the Australians have had to plan for playing cricket. They have planned and prepared the artificial pitch that in one form or another serves both picnic games in the bush and the Test Match. They have channelled their talents of play in elaborate and far-reaching administration. They have cultivated a seaborne seed to a crop of cricketing eminence.'

This distinctiveness became apparent as the colonies grew. Where Sydney led Tasmania, or, as it was in those days, Van Diemen's Land, followed. Then Perth, Adelaide, Melbourne and Brisbane. The 'tyranny of distance' between

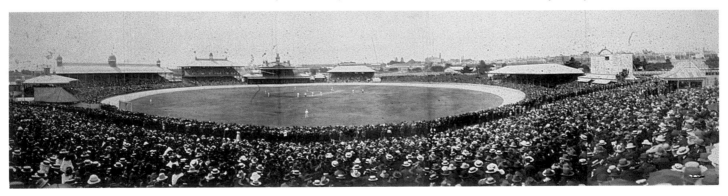

each settlement restricted quick inter-state progress. In March 1856, however the first match between Victoria and New South Wales took place at the newly converted Richmond Paddock. Fairfax and Biers' *Australian Cricketer's Guide* was soon forthcoming, to be followed in time by similar offerings from Hammersley, Wills and Whitridge. The stimulus of a tour from two English sides in short succession, Heathfield Stephenson's of 1861–62 and George Parr's of 1863–64, accelerated an improvement in standards. "Well, oi don' think mooch of their play, but they're a wonderful lot of drinkin' men!" opined Roger Iddison after the first visit. Very soon the quality of Australian play was to match the quantity of players' intake. The Test Match era arrived, titanic matches ensued, controversies came and went, the Ashes were consigned to a velvet bag made by Annie Fletcher after a spectator died of excitement at Australia's historic victory, the Earl of Sheffield donated the prestigious and handsome domestic cricket trophy, tours to and from England became commonplace and such cricketers as Bannerman, Blackham, Bonnor, Giffen, Murdoch, Spofforth and Turner were to become legends in their own time. Then came Trumper, whose performances 'sparkled like crown jewels' and whose ill-health and early death thankfully spared him having to suffer the sort of jealous denigration that often seems unfairly reserved for those whose careers run the full course. His fluent mastery over all types of bowling affirmed a player of exceptional gifts.

The horizon of Australia's touring itinerary widened to include South Africa in 1902. Ugly stormclouds presaged the 1912 visit to British shores for the Triangular Tournament with a dispute over the right to appoint a manager. Eleven Test Match victories over England marked a period of ascendancy between 1920 and 1925. Perfect batting pitches spawned massive totals, Victoria taxing the stamina of the scorers with an innings total of 1,107. Then came the arrival of Bradman, who seemed unassailable and whose achievements are forever likely to be unmatched. A pause just to reflect on the implication and ratio of his incredible run-accumulation is not out of place. They are reproduced from Irving Rosenwater's omniscient biography and based on statistics given in a publication of the Australian Broadcasting Commission:

|  | Inns. | N.O. | Runs | H.S. | Av. | 100s |
|---|---|---|---|---|---|---|
| First-class cricket | 338 | 43 | 28,067 | 452* | 95.14 | 117 |
| Minor cricket | 331 | 64 | 22,664 | 320* | 84.88 | 94 |
|  | 669 | 107 | 50,731 | 452* | 90.26 | 211 |

At a glance we can see that over a third of Bradman's first class innings resulted in centuries. A breakdown of the magical three figures then reveals that one exceeded four hundred, five topped three hundred and no fewer than thirty-one surpassed two hundred.

Too much has been written about the 'bodyline' saga beyond the need to note its happenings. That particularly unhappy series of engagements was the only Test rubber lost to England in the 1930s, during which connoisseurs of spin-bowling were spoilt for choice between Grimmett, O'Reilly and Fleetwood-Smith. The decade also witnessed the first round of rubbers against the West Indies and the fifth and sixth series between Australia and South Africa. Though the South Africans had only one glorious Test victory to show for much endeavour there were signs of real progress since the turn of the century, when the initial invitation to the Australians to take part in three Test matches has

An extraordinary scorecard. Only the second innings of a thousand or more in first-class cricket, though Victoria's total may have been exceeded in a minor game in Australia some fifty or so years earlier. The scoring details of that occasion, however, are haphazard and inconsistent.

been regarded as 'tantamount to asking Kreisler to play in a suburban orchestra'.

Having been sired by soldiery, cricket started to become established in South Africa with the formation of a club at Port Elizabeth in 1843. The game was also played in Pietermaritzburg and Cape Town, and by the 1860s a train of Mother Country *v* Colonial-Born matches was under way. In 1876 there was the first 'Champion Bat' trophy, involving teams from Cape Town, Grahamstown, King William's Town and Port Elizabeth, to be followed by similar tournaments that included other domains like Kimberley during the 1880s.

Major Warton's team, captained by C. Aubrey Smith, had an eventful and eminently successful first tour in 1888/89, mostly destroying inferior opposition, who often fielded twice as many players, on matting or solid mud wickets. Two so-called 'Tests' were played, the Currie Cup was inaugurated and three more tours visited the Veldt, before the century closed. South Africa reciprocated with journeys to England, though for the first venture, in 1894, the omission of J. 'Krom' Hendricks, the Cape Malay fast bowler, sounded ominous overtones. Hendricks and L. Sammodien had both performed wonderfully well shortly before against W.W. Read's English side, in the only fixture that has

A depleted England team lost the series 4–1. The captain, A.O. Jones, was indisposed for much of the tour and missed three tests.

*In the Nets*, Laurence Toynbee. About half of Toynbee's output is sporting material – rugger, football, tennis, golf and squash, all have received attention besides cricket. It is fairly safe to assume that he has captured more cricketing moments on canvas than any other artist. Toynbee himself played the game for Ampleforth, Oxford and M.C.C. In an article for the *Yorkshire Post*, Michael Hickling noted that 'the ambition behind his sporting subjects is to capture a fleeting instant in a contest when the strainings of a group of players are frozen in a rhythmic composition'. He seeks not to record a match as through the eye of a camera, but rather the split second of shutter speed, an 'elusive and intangible quality, the apotheosis of movement'.

ever taken place between a 'black' side and an international touring team. Incidentally, concurrent with the organization of white provincial cricket, the game for blacks also flourished in inter-town tournaments and mixed matches before the semi-liberal policies prevailing in the Cape Colony ceased in 1910. The non-whites have functioned independently as a centralized body for the Barnato Trophy and then separately in various groupings for other cups.

Representing South Africa at Test level over the years have been many outstanding players whose deeds have a deserved place in cricket's pantheon: the Nourse's, A.W. 'Dave' and son Dudley, a doughty captain, who grittily compiled a double century with a broken thumb to win a Test match; Bruce Mitchell, prolific run-getter; spinner Xenophon Balaskas, whose skill secured South Africa's first Test win over England away from home; the Rowan brothers, Eric, reliable opening bat and Athol, a classy off-spinner; 'Tufty' Mann; Jackie McGlew; Roy McLean, Hugh Tayfield; Trevor Goddard; the Pollocks; Colin Bland; Barlow, Bacher, Richards, Procter – the names lustrous and for many their performance incomplete. The D'Oliveira affair expedited a schism in sporting concourse and the subsequent 'rebel' tours have left a broken bridge yet to be satisfactorily mended.

The Southern part of the African continent is now represented in competition abroad by Zimbabwe, with noteworthy success in the ICC Trophy and a recent startling one-day victory over Australia in the World Cup. Cricket was first heard of in Rhodesia, as it was then known, in 1890, and in the century since, many Rhodesians have played for the South African Test side, including Percy Mansell, Colin Bland, the Pitneys. Jackie du Preez and A.J. Traicios. The Zimbabwean national team play to a very high standard, and it may not be long before they are granted full status.

The West Indies, that glittering necklace of islands stretching from the most easterly in the chain, Barbados – where there has been a greater concentration of enthusiastic expertise than in any other comparably confined geographical location – to Jamaica, the largest of the territories some thousand miles away, provide a never-ending flow of charismatic cricketers. Whenever they play abroad, their coruscating strokes, lethal bowling, brilliant catches and lissome throws are redolent of sunny skies, lambent lagoons with swirling undercurrents, tropical palms, calypsos and rum punch. The very names of a clutch of starry strikers radiate a sense of sheer abandonment and a complete lack of inhibition: Ollivierre, Walcott, Weekes, Sobers, Kanhai, Kallicharan, Lloyd and Richards. The story of Caribbean cricket in much of the last decade and a half has been one of unstoppable success.

The growth of the game in the West Indies owed much to tours led by pioneers like Lord Hawke and 'Plum' Warner, although there had been exchanges with North America prior to their advent in the 1890s. Warner had an affinity for the islands and their people, as is evidenced in a broadcast talk that he gave:

'My first recollections of cricket are of playing in my nightshirt on a marble gallery in Trinidad at half-past six in the morning. I was bowled to by a boy by the name of Killibree, which, in the patois of Trinidad means humming-bird. Armed with my little bat, I sometimes broke the windows of the rooms looking on to the gallery and I got quite used to my father's remark: "There's that wretched boy again!" It was always countered by Killibree assuring him that "Mr. Pelham he make a good batsman, sir, when he grow big, sir".'

The dynamic Learie Constantine, unorthodox hitter, dangerous fast bowler who could strike like an anaconda and a fielder of amazing simian propensities,

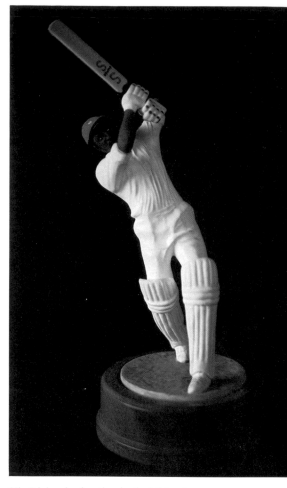

Viv Richards. Another in the D'Aquino series. The Polish-born Count was inspired to embark on the project by his Alderney neighbour – John Arlott.

(*Opposite*) A cure for seasickness.

took the same dusty track to the top as many a compatriot. He learned his first cricket on a cocoa estate in Trinidad with a sun-dried orange for a ball, a bat made from a coconut tree and the kitchen crockery used to practise catches. Constantine, more than any other West Indian, with the possible later exception of Sobers, could win a match on his own. His electrifyingly quick response to any situation stood him in favourable stead in retirement when he entered politics and was awarded first a knighthood, then a Life Peerage.

Constantine's father, L.S., was chosen for the first visit to England in 1900. 'Old Cons' could not afford the trip and on the day that the boat left he was found idling disconsolately downtown. A remarkably hasty public whip-round took place, a fast launch was chartered and the now jubilant Constantine hauled aboard the boat in the Gulf of Paria. His Boys Own adventure was crowned with a century at Lord's against MCC, the first West Indian hundred in England.

Nowadays West Indian cricket is inextricably associated with a four-pronged pace attack but it is not too many years since they entered Tests on a regular basis with at least a modicum of spin. Lance Gibbs, a looping off-spinner with many subtle variations of flight, tremendously effective on a hard wicket and the second international bowler to achieve three hundred wickets in Tests, had a long and distinguished career. And Roger Harper, the current incumbent, is no tyro, yet one feels that his potential has not yet been fully exploited. Then there were the spin-twins, Ramadhin and Valentine, who had so many permutations at their disposal during the 1950 tour that for much of the series the English batting seemed permanently paralyzed. It has to be accepted nevertheless that the intrinsic excitement and histrionics of extreme pace are attuned to the Caribbean temperament. The sight of loose-limbed fiery fast bowlers preparing to unleash a bomb-pack in the manner of a Barnes Wallis creation against the Mohne Dam has galvanic effect. From Martindale, Hylton, Johnson, Gilchrist, Hall and Griffith to the neoteric platoons of Holding, Roberts, Croft, Garner and Marshall, batsmen have been bruised by the bouncer. Sometimes the bowlers have been firing at sides demoralized by large totals accumulated by talented run-getters like George Headley, Jeffrey Stollmeyer, Frank Worrell, Conrad Hunte, Desmond Haynes and Gordon Greenidge. More often than not

(*Previous page left*) A precarious perch for Jamaican enthusiasts at the first Test against England, Kingston, 1986.

(*Previous page right*) Keeping an eye on the ball. School cricket in Barbados.

Cricket at Boston, Massachusetts, U.S.A. in 1859 and reproduced by Winslow Horner in Ballou's *Pictorial Drawing-room Companion*.

A printed cardboard breakfast menu which contained caricatures of the players by Kerwin Macgrath, each signed by the subject.

(*Next pages*) The craftsmen at work.

it is they themselves who have undermined the opposition and the batsmen who have reaped the rewards.

It was no whimsical indulgence that led the West Indians to the American continent for their first venture abroad in 1886. Canada and the USA had been playing one another in regular exchanges since 1844 in what is generally believed to be the oldest international sporting fixture in the world. The first tour from England, in 1859, had gone to North America – their adventurous forays into the nether regions clad in greatcoats and mufflers are industriously recounted by Frederick Lillywhite – and there had been five subsequent visits by the time the West Indies went to Canada.

Philadelphia became the focus of American cricket in the last quarter of the nineteenth century and the years before World War I with a succession of games against the national sides then operating. Perhaps the Philadelphians' most memorable victory was against the Australian team in 1893, when the margin of victory was so conclusive – an innings and 68 runs. The Philadelphians amassed 525 in their sole innings. In J. Barton King they had a truly accomplished bowler, one of the great in-swingers of all time who could deliver a ball described as an 'angler' which would change direction sharply and very late. In 1908 King headed the first-class English bowling averages. The decline of cricket in America has been ascribed to many things, not least the temperament of a nation housing a multitude of different races and a plethora of sporting counter-attractions.

It was also in the 1880s that a side representing a community in the Indian sub-continent visited England twice. The Parsees had formed their own club on the Esplanade Maidan in Bombay in 1848, calling it the Orient, and had persevered with the game commendably in the face of daunting odds, notably, lack of proper equipment. Their first tour, in 1886, brought but one victory in twenty-eight matches, however such was the Parsees' enthusiasm that they made another trip two years later and were rewarded with eight wins in thirty-one games. Now an expected pattern of reciprocal tours followed. G.F. Vernon and the ubiquitous Lord Hawke led prelusory bands and it was not many years before competitive cricket on a domestic level started to spread in India. The feats of Ranjitsinghi in England were relayed back home and fellow princes fostered cricket in their own states. Seeing the zeal of the Europeans and the Parsees, the Hindus and the Mohammedans were converted to the attractions of the game and competitions were arranged. An All-India side under the Maharaja of Patiala toured England in 1911. The lifestyle of His Highness had been portrayed as being 'influenced by the *Tales of the Arabian Nights*' and he is remembered 'as a burly Sikh who wore a large diamond earring and hit straight sixes with great power'. Apparently the diamond earring helped the tour's social success, but there were insufficient sixes to ensure the equivalent on the field. By the time of the 1926 MCC visit to India under Arthur Gilligan, the situation had somewhat altered. The general standard had improved, a Board of Control for Cricket in India was soon to be elected, another tour took place and finally, in 1932, a three-day Test at Lord's was forthcoming. Yet another nation had joined the confederation of top level cricketing countries. C.K. Nayudu captained India in that maiden Test and Mohammed Nissar and Amar Singh, fast and medium respectively, excelled themselves with the ball.

It took India a long time to find its feet internationally, which is not to say that they have lacked individual players with great flair. Vijay Merchant, Mushtaq Ali, V.S. Hazare, Lala Amarnath and Vinoo Mankad come to mind immedi-

Victor Trumper by Judith Dobie.
Realized from the Beldam photograph.

ately, the last two outstanding all-rounders, the first three formidable batsmen. Spinners Subash Gupte and Chandu Borde, and in later years Bishen Bedi, Chandrasekhar, Prasanna and Venkataraghavan, bamboozled many a batsman with their wiles. It is only in the last few years though that Indian cricket has really flowered. The inherent weaknesses of the system – too many state sides not worthy of a place in the Ranji Trophy and an over-abundance of drawn games, with captains preferring stalemate to the risk of trying to force a victory – seems to have been surmounted, or perhaps more accurately, sidestepped. Whatever the reason, the princely talents of Visnawath, Vengsarkar, Gavaskar and Kapil Dev escaped being stultified and instead, honed by a perpetual round of international engagements, have glowed over the cricketing world. Their success has inspired their colleagues, and with the added confidence gained from a World Cup victory India now starts practically any Test series with a better than even chance.

Pakistan, founded as such in 1947, wasted no time in displaying their credentials. Within five years of being accorded Test status in 1952 they had achieved victories over England, Australia, New Zealand and, for them most satisfyingly, India. An outstanding captain, Abdul Hafeez Kardar, a great bowler, Fazal Mahmood, a wicket-keeper batsman of aplomb, Imtiaz Ahmed, an opening batsman of inexhaustible patience, Hanif Mohammed, his brother Mushtaq, an exhilarating all-rounder – these were Pakistan's early heroes. They were succeeded by others: Majid Khan, Asif Iqbal, Wasim Bari, Intikhab Alam, Zaheer Abbas, Sarfraz Nawaz, Javed Miandad and, of course, Imran Khan. Characteristics of Pakistani cricket are the boundless flair richly distributed among their players, internecine squabbling at selection level and questionable umpiring.

After a brutal war the eastern wing of Pakistan became an independent Bangladesh in 1973. The Bangladeshis have yet to establish themselves on the world cricketing stage, which is hardly surprising in a nation racked by human and natural disaster. They have taken part in the ICC Trophy and several of their players have shown promise, none more so that Ashraful Haq, who took 7 for 23 with cleverly flighted off-spinners against Fiji in the 1979 competition. Given regular exposure to top-class cricket, continual encouragement and ready financial resources, there is no reason why Bangladesh should not eventually follow Sri Lanka, the latest country to be decorated with the full Test Match insignia.

Sri Lanka, or as it was, Ceylon, has a cricket history going back to the year before Nyren was first published. In 1832 the first club was formed, which is usually a case of consensus as a result of playing on a haphazard basis before the idea materialized. During the nineteenth century eager planters neglected their coffee to trek as much as thirty miles through the jungle before putting bat to ball on levelled-out hillside terrain that could be over six thousand feet above sea level. There were several European *v* Ceylonese matches in the later 1800s and it was then that touring sides started the practise of a 'whistle-stop' game in Colombo en route to Australia or England.

The Ceylon Cricket Association was founded a few years after World War I and gradually longer visits to the island took place. The journey towards official Test recognition was protracted, and it was not until the 1980s, after winning the inaugural ICC Trophy in 1979 and with a victory over India and steady performances elsewhere, that the goal was reached. Between the two World Wars C.H. Gunasekera, F.C. de Saram and S.S. Jayawickrema were leading players, and more recently Michael Tissera, Stanley Jayasinghe, Annura Tennekoon, Duleep Mendis and Sunil Wettimuny have made names for themselves. Now, as Sri Lanka, the Test side have proved they are nobody's pushovers, with several of their frontline batsmen being admired for stylish stroke-making in the classical tradition. If only they can acquire more penetration in the attack the all-round strength of the side will increase immeasurably.

Sri Lanka's long peregrination towards Test standing has been equalled, if nor surpassed, by that of New Zealand. In *Barclay's World of Cricket* T.P. McLean quotes the 'Rosetti, who asked: "Does the road wind uphill all the way?" and who herself answered: "Yes, to the very end."' He continues, she 'could be said to have uttered an exact and prophetic statement as to the game in cricket's southernmost seas. In the nigh on one hundred and forty years during which it has faithfully been followed and played in New Zealand, ninety were spent in achieving Test Match status.' In retrospect, that may appear surprising, though bearing in mind New Zealand's place on the map and its relative contiguity to Australia, one can quickly understand why it is not so. Before the phenomenon of air travel the distance, time and expense involved in getting to Australasia meant that tourists usually finished their visit with the New Zealand 'leg' as a make-weight. In fact even nowadays that is still often the case. Therefore New Zealand has suffered historically from being a kind of poor relation.

Some authorities give the first cricket match in the colony as that at Russell, by the Bay of Islands, in 1842, and state that the game was then played in Wellington, Dunedin and Christchurch. Here again, though, those hardy settlers are likely to have knocked a ball around before the earliest recorded encounter. In March 1860 the first inter-provincial contest occurred – a challenge between Wellington and Auckland – and then four years later Parr's England team visited 'and gave a great fillip to the game'.

It was not until 1894 that the New Zealand Cricket Council was established

*Middlesex at Dartford.* Judith Dobie's individual study of 1985. One of a limited edition of 20.

Studies in concentration. The Long
Room at Lords. Dennis Flanders, 1953.

Dennis Flanders. 1953.

and then, a dozen years after that, the Plunket Shield inaugurated. The Shield, for domestic competition, was donated by Lord Plunket, the Governor-General. Tours came and went – one of the longest to the country before World War I was by an English team captained by P.F. Warner – and New Zealanders continued to play their cricket for most of the time 'free of the grimmer aspects of the professional game'. Don Neely and Richard King, in their comprehensive history of New Zealand International Cricket, 1894–1985, *Men in White*, expand on the point. 'Perhaps at some cost to its win-loss ratio in international matches the sport has until recently enjoyed an aura of amateur innocence. This came about more from necessity than choice – this country's small population inhibited the growth of professional cricket – but it did result in New Zealand touring teams receiving praise for their sportsmanship and a sunny adventurous disposition.'

Undoubtedly New Zealand cricket reached its nadir one afternoon in 1955 at Eden Park, Auckland, when Statham, Tyson and Appleyard dismissed them for 26 in the second innings, but almost exactly one year later they at last scaled the peak they had perhaps thought unattainable. In front of seven thousand delirious souls, New Zealand humbled the mighty West Indians and recorded their first ever Test victory. All that a former captain, Geoff Rabone, could say, repeatedly, was: 'I'm so bloody pleased. I'm so bloody pleased.'

In recent years New Zealand have more often held their own internationally, due principally to the towering talents of all-rounder Richard Hadlee. Hadlee, one of three brothers to play for his country – his father, Walter, was captain just after the War – has been a dynamic force for whichever side he plays.

Many New Zealanders have graced cricket pitches around the world with a high degree of distinctive skill, notably T.C. Lowry; the Vivians, father and son; Bert Sutcliffe; Martin Donnelly; John Reid; Glenn Turner and the brothers Crowe. Today's New Zealand Test cricketer generally plays with the sophistication some of his predecessors lacked, and there would be little comparison with the game to which Charles Darwin referred when Maoris played at Waivate at Christmastime in 1835. That note gives a cue to the indigenous population of neighbouring Australia and the spectacular, if ill-fated, Aborigine tour of England in 1868, repeated much more happily and with some success one hundred years later.

It is true to say there is scarcely a part of the globe that has not witnessed cricket in one form or another: every continent – including Antarctica, up mountain, down valley, on sea and on land, on beach and on pavement, outdoors and indoors. In South America, where British prisoners-of-war played in 1806, and Argentina by 1980 had conducted eighty-eight tours in one hundred and eleven years, including sixty-six against such other Latin American countries as Brazil, Uruguay and Chile. Then, moving up-country to Central America, specifically Nicaragua, we find that an old cricketer wrote in 1886: 'I have instituted your favourite old game, cricket, among the natives, but they are such a lazy race that half-an-hour of it at a spin completely does them up'. Further north in Guatemala there was a proposal to send a team to British Honduras in 1909 one year after Isaiah Thomas had issued a pamphlet in Belize entitled *A Concise Hint and Guide to Cricket*, while in Panama there was issued a special cricket number of *The Tribune* to commemorate the visit of the West Indies team on their way to tour Australia, 1930/31. In Mexico too the capital boasted a club as early as 1838, and later teams included Pachuca, Velasco, Reforma, Monterrey and Rancheros of Muzquiz.

Richard Hadlee about to unleash yet another lethal delivery.

The New Norcia Aboriginal side, Western Australia, 1879. Reproduced from *The Graphic*.

(*Next page left*) Australia v. England at Sydney, 1983.

(*Next page right*) An aerial view of the splendidly well-appointed ground in Sharjah, United Arab Emirates, 1984.

In Asia, a similar picture unfolds. Games took place in Hong Kong in 1840 while matches between the Crown Colony and Shanghai date back to 1866 and between China and Japan to 1893. King Thebaw of Burma was fascinated by cricket, and woe betide anybody who dismissed him. The Amir of Afghanistan cultivated slogging in Kabul, ready with a corresponding 'use of injurious language' for anyone foolish enough to bowl a ball that could not be hit. Not that cricket was a prerogative of the ruling class in either country.

Malaysia and Singapore have entertained many international sides with spacious grounds in the former and a picturesque environment in the latter. The game in Singapore goes back in records to 1837.

The Bangkok City, the first known cricket club in Thailand, previously Siam, was formed in 1890, probably as a direct result of upper-class Thai children receiving an education in England.

Elsewhere the game has a voice in West Africa, with competitive exchanges between Nigeria, Ghana, Sierra Leone and The Gambia – there is also a league in Liberia – and short visits from MCC sides. In East Africa as well – Kenya, Uganda and Tanzania – where originally cricket was a pastime for the settlers, again MCC have made frequent excursions. There have also been visits to Zambia. During the 1960s there was a pioneering tour of Ethiopia by Australian schoolboy cricketers, though the desperate struggle to merely stay alive in many parts of that country at the moment is likely to preclude any thought of further sporting endeavour.

In Egypt cricket fell in line behind polo, though each year for a decade from 1929, H.M. Martineau's team, including many prominent players, embarked

(*Left*) Dennis Lillee by Count André D'Aquino.

(*Right*) A match at Selangor, Malaysia.

for a tour lasting a month. The Alexandria Club, founded in 1851, and the Gezira Sporting Club were the two main hosts for visiting combinations, and it should not be forgotten that an Egyptian side came to England in 1951 and played MCC at Lord's, with actor Omar Sharif in the party.

During the last few years cricket has found a home in a most unlikely venue. Due to the enthusiastic support of Abdul Rehman Bukhatir, a huge stadium has been built in the Emirate of Sharjah, where challenge competitions and the First Asian Cup have taken place.

Israel, despite British influence, waited until 1966 to organize a cricket league that comprised ten clubs. Games are played on matting wickets and, considering the hostile force of nature in that part of the world, it is little short of a miracle that the national side performed so creditably in ICC Trophy games.

The dictates of space deny us any more globe-trotting. How pleasant it would have been to linger in Fiji where cricket in calf-length skirts has been long established and where once, from the minuscule island of Bau, a side chosen from the sixty-strong male population left to tour Australia. A splendid book by Philip Snow, *Cricket in the Fiji Islands*, threads together expertly the Fijians' colourful cricketing history and informs us that one of their most gifted players possessed the longest surname in the game, Talebulamaineiilike-namainavelaniveivakabulaimainakulalakeba. The South seas have, as well, other attractions. Papua New Guinea fielded seven indigenous players to beat the West Indies in 1977, and cricket is played too in the Solomon Islands, the New Hebrides and memorably, in Samoa, where entire districts of two to three hundred aside have played games that stretched on interminably. Then there is New Caledonia, where women dressed in 'highly-coloured, knee-length Mother Hubbards .. with straw hats and frangipani flowers' play an animated version of cricket with much cut and thrust. We could go on and on, from Mauritius, with cricket in existence in 1838, to the Yemen, to Nepal, to St. Helena and to Tristan da Cunha . . .

Any game that can persuade its practitioners to have its laws translated into Greek (care of Christopher Box-Grainger) – Corfiot cricket is attracting an ever-expanding library to account for the numerous encounters on the Esplanade – or manufacture bat and stumps from the jaw-bone and ribs of a stranded whale in arctic Greenland has to have an eccentric appeal that defies national boundaries.

# The Modern Era

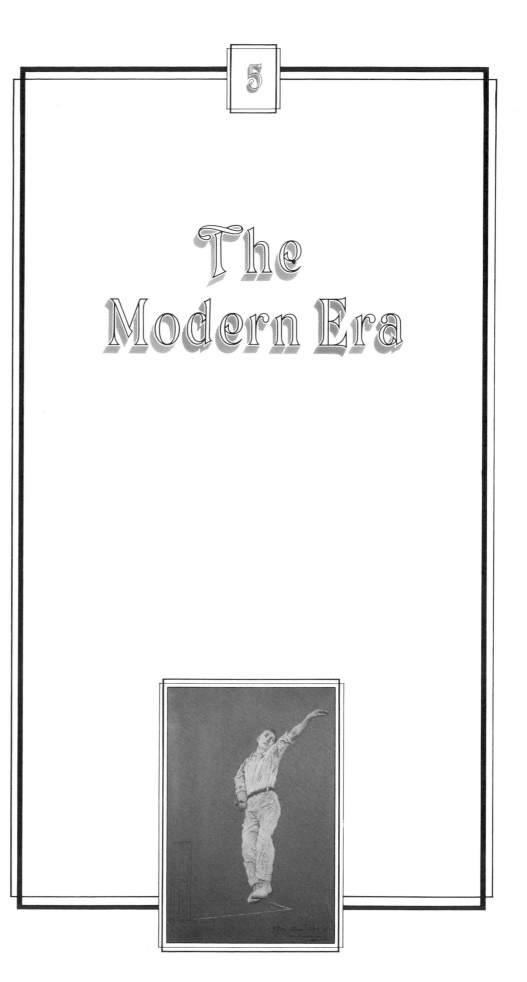

(*Previous page*) Larry Smart's vivid depiction of cricket at St. Mary's Grange, Wiltshire.

Instantly recognizable effervescent flourishes by Ralph Steadman.

The rebirth of professional cricket in England after World War II was both a joyous and painful experience. The joy of players and spectators in taking part in and watching such a harmonious pursuit as cricket after the savage discordances of a the recent past was overt. The pain at yet again having snatched away by time or trigger a cherished cricketing kinsman was more concealed.

The love of the game was unabated. Service elevens and makeshift teams had played whenever and wherever they could; prisoners-of-war had even produced their own cricketers' magazine – at Eichstätt in Germany – formulating matches to distract the guards while tunnelling went on beneath their feet; and, with priorities in exactly the right place, *Wisden* had not only survived the blitz but had issued a most useful index to their editions to date. In the foreword to that index Harry Altham quoted a passage from Arthur Bryant's *English Saga*, which was reflecting on the 'complex – and to the foreigner no doubt unintelligible – amalgam of loyalties, enthusiasms and associations' challenged by Germany in the previous conflict of 1914.

'Behind the easy façade of England,' wrote Bryant, 'there was something mightier than England: there was Hayward and Hobbs going in to bat, the Oddfellows' dinner and the Old Kent Road.' Not much had changed.

In 1946, the cobwebs and rust were brushed from pavilion doors and trusty holdalls in preparation for a new dawn. Inevitably, with such teeming expectancy, the weather was wet. In fact, the whole session could be regarded as a prolonged practice session for the following year, when at last 'sumer (was) icumen in'.

Nineteen forty-seven is synonymous with Compton and Edrich. Under glorious blue skies the sporting nation could forget the rigours of the ration book and luxuriate in the mastery of bat over ball. The record books relay the astonishing statistics that accrued from Denis's brilliant unorthodoxy and Bill's gutsy rusticity.

The following two years saw English cricket steam-rollered by Bradman's all-conquering Australians, then undergoing necessary sedation from the relatively placid New Zealanders before starting on the road to resurgence with the 1950 visit of the West Indians. The exhilarating strokes of Walcott, Weekes and Worrell and the wily spinning of Ramadkin and Valentine were too much for their opponents, but they provoked a determination to find a new footing.

Two pictures melded into one. L.S.
Lowry's view of Lancashire League
amidst factory grime.

The first professional captain of the national side was appointed, Leonard Hutton assuming another mantle which must often have been burdensome in the extreme. 'As an England and Yorkshire batsman from 1946 to the end of his career he was always the first objective of enemy assault, and experience taught him that he represented only only the protective moat and curtain wall but often enough the keep as well,' considered Jim Kilburn.

Help though, was at hand. Pubescent lions were ready to pounce. May and Cowdrey strengthened the batting, Trueman and Statham spearheaded the bowling and Laker and Lock stood by as a second besieging force. The resolution and accuracy of Bedser had found new support, Tyson shattered defences with sheer speed and Bailey broke bowlers' hearts with stickle stonewalling. The Ashes were recovered and retained. Pakistan became the only side to win a Test match on a first visit to England, and England in turn won a series in the West Indies for the very first time.

After holding two records for nearly twenty years, Hutton, now Sir Leonard and retired from Test cricket, lost them both in a matter of weeks. His batting time for the longest innings in first-class cricket was superseded by Hanif Mohammed and his highest score in Text cricket was passed by Garfield Sobers.

On the domestic scene Surrey had the greatest unbroken successful run in the history of the County Championship, a monopoly over seven seasons. Their resources were enviable: the penetrative bowling of the Bedsers, Laker, Lock and Loader, high-class batting from May, Barrington and Stewart, the agile wicket-keeping of McIntyre, an incredible all-round fielding ability, especially close to the wicket, and the inspirational captaincy of Stuart Surridge.

In-swing bowling dominated cricket. Batting was constrained and matches

A gold stick-pin. The bat is set with a solitaire diamond in a case.

(*Right*) Continental Spelter statuette, probably Belgian, circa 1905, possibly based on C.B. Fry.

(*Below*) Doctoring the pitch at dead of night. Some covert conspirators. At least twice in recent years the turf has been tampered with by those with axes to grind.

(*Right*) 'Ranji and the Champion'. A painted wood carving by Howard Carter, whose childhood spent around sawmills and timber yards gave him a respect and liking for the material. Carter's work, a number of humorous depictions of sporting heroes and in which he often uses pine, turpentine, shellac and gesso, combines qualities of folk art with elements of an academic tradition.

(*Left*) From banknote to beermats.

(*Below*) Three-dimensional wire and paper collage by Kathryn Jackson, 1988.

became attritional. The malady was only partly relieved by minor changes in the laws. Attendances declined and by the early 1960s there were serious doubts as to the long-term continuance of the County Championship. Many were the suggestions put to find a fresh format. One plan, devised in 1960 by Charles Jones, who had organized the London Counties team during World War II, proposed thirty three-day Tests between England, Australia, New Zealand, India and Pakistan, staged at each of the seventeen first-class county 'homes'. The County Championship itself would be reduced to sixteen matches with no return fixtures. 'I feel sure,' said Mr. Jones, 'that three-day Test matches with the world's leading personalities taking part could be the answer to putting cricket back on its feet again.'

The idea was never adopted, though it is easy to detect a common seed for the afternoon jaunts by the International Cavaliers that attracted the television cameras a few years later, and also eventually the birth of a World Cup for Cricket.

The game, seeking solvency, secured a future through sponsorship, and in the last twenty or so years companies such as Rothman's, Gillette, John Player, Benson and Hedges, Schweppes, Britannic Assurance, Cornhill, Texaco, Tilcon and Asda have given their names to a variety of competition. The National Westminster Bank and Refuge Assurance also entered the lists, and the limited-

(*Above*) The 1954/55 English tourists to Australasia caricatured on wood.

(*Left*) A trial design for the souvenir programme of the 1948 Australian tour.

(*Right*) Geoff Howarth just regaining his ground in an indoor game at Wembley Arena. Farokh Engineer is the wicket-keeper.

(*Next page left*) Imran Khan ready to strike.

(*Next page right*) The personification of power. Botham in his pomp.

The inscription reads that The Wisden Trophy, 'to be competed for between England and West Indies in 1963 and succeeding Test Series, was presented by Wisden's to commemorate the publication in 1963 of the 100th edition of Wisden's Cricketers' Almanack.'

over game, ranging from sixty (originally sixty-five) to forty overs per side, not only wooed back the old disenchanted watcher but also seduced a new one.

There was, however, a price to pay. The popularity of limited-over cricket, the added strains of a seven-days-a-week commitment to diametrically differing games, and fundamentally the rising cost of living allied to poor remuneration caused financial unrest among the players.

Suddenly the underground ferment found focus. Amid the hospitality-tent gorgers of factory-farmed chicken and guzzled champagne was being chirrupped a new name. Not just a paper tiger but an archetypal anti-hero for the established order, tycoon Kerry Packer. The real reason for the Australian entrepreneur's intrusion into cricket soon became apparent: not so much to provide an alternative source of employment for the players but rather to secure television rights for prestigious games. Even so, if there had been fewer Test-class players around the world left in a vacuum through the politics surrounding South Africa, it would not have been easy to raise such high-calibre teams. World Series Cricket persuaded the likes of Asif Iqbal, Imran Khan, Mushtaq Mohammed, Eddie Barlow, Mike Procter, Barry Richards, Graeme Pollock, Vivian Richards, Clive Lloyd, Alan Knott, Derek Underwood and John Snow, among other notable names, to sign contracts. Tony Greig, Packer's chief negotiator, was accused of 'disembowelling' world cricket.

The enormous public interest evoked by the 'Packer Affair' was only part of an increased commercial awareness of the game that manifested itself in all sorts of ways. The collecting bug has been well catered for. Shortly after the auction sale of part of the legendary J.W. Goldman's library of cricket books in 1966, the doyen of bibliographical cricketing matters, Leslie Gutteridge, who for many years had presided at Epworth's in the City Road, emigrated to Canada. In his wake there came E.K. Brown in Cornwall and J.W. McKenzie in Surrey, who produced catalogues of books for sale of a quality not seen before. Martin Wood, in Kent, was another with an international mailing list. All of them were following a long tradition, begun individually by Gaston in the nineteenth century, that had spread to the firm of Cotterell's in Birmingham in the 1930s

(Below) An elegant mover. The Caribbean's cricketing Knight – Sir Garfield Sobers, kept in check by Alan Knott, at Lords, 1973.

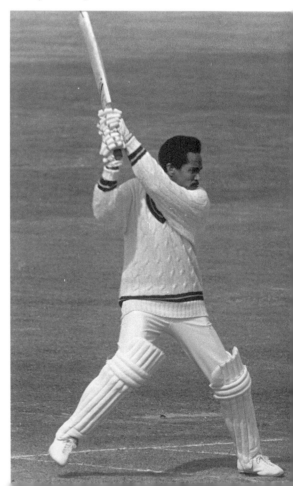

(*Next page left*) Mulish mowing of the outfield for the third Test Match between Pakistan and England at Karachi in 1978.

(*Next page right*) The roar of the greasepaint, the smell of the crowd. Backstage at the second Test Match between India and England at New Delhi in 1984.

(*Right*) An airborne Kapil Dev during the second Test Match between India and England at New Delhi, 1984.

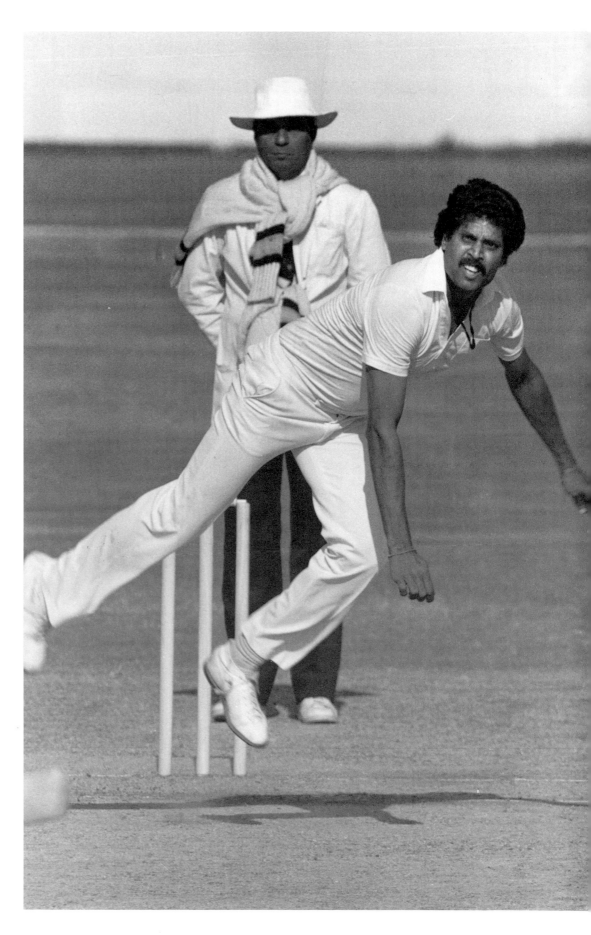

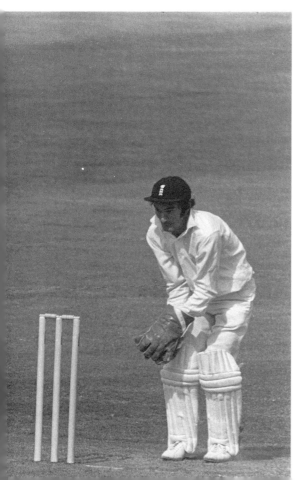

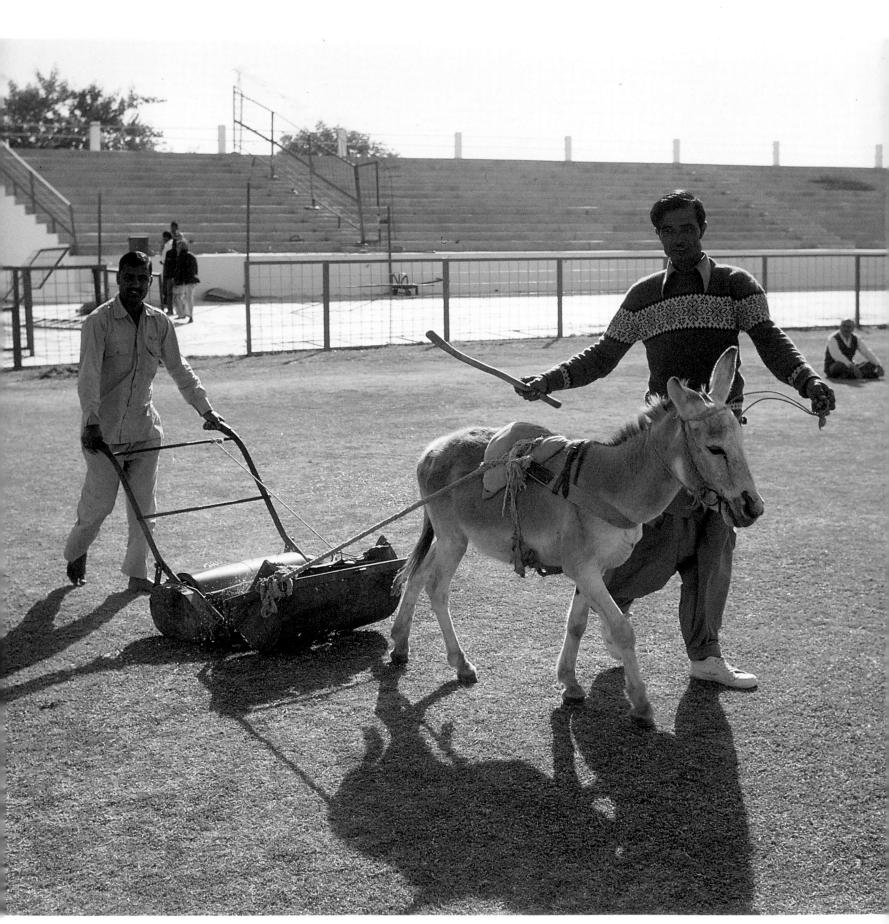

and then to Epworth's post-war. There have been many other significant sellers along the way. Latterly, the artistic side of cricket has been exhibited most attractively by Nicholas Potter at the Burlington Gallery in London.

During the 1970s and early '80s, the price for a set of *Wisden*'s rapidly multiplied many times. The auctioneers Phillips began to hold bi-annual sales at which anything and everything with a cricketing motif, from matchbox labels to mezzotints, went for prices guaranteed to cause heads to shake in wonderment. Rival houses like Christies and, to a lesser extent, Bonham's and Sotheby's copied their success. Even the MCC could not afford to remain aloof, and in 1987, via Christie's, sold some of their reserve collection in an auction at Lord's that lasted eleven and a half hours and was dubbed 'The Sale of the Double Century'.

The marketing of cricket and its impedimenta now knows no bounds: lambswool sweaters, crystal decanters, paperweights, dice and card games, hip flasks, place-mats, tea-towels and children's teddy bears, all designed with the game's followers as targets, are to be found on stall or in shop at the periphery of nearly every county ground.

Another indication of cricket's commercial potential is in the extent to which the entertainment business has discovered another stage for charitable causes. In a sense the Lord's Taverners are an extension of the Thespids, the Stage XI and many similar outfits who through the years indulged themselves and their audiences with artless bowling and dicky batting. Their difference is that the organization is run professionally with a commendable *raison d'être*.

A less palatable aspect of the modernization of cricket is the behaviour of some of the crowd. The reaction to yet another extraordinary feat against the clock or number of deliveries, as yet another trophy is held aloft on the pavilion balcony at Lord's, is boorish and bodes ill for the future. The baying and beer-can banging, the chanting and the running on to the field at the first opportunity, have many of the hallmarks of football hooliganism, and are timely reminders that cricket has now gone full circle from the early days, when betting on matches was regularly accompanied by disturbances.

Traditionalists find it increasingly hard to come to terms with recent expositions of today's social climate and the way it has affected their beloved game. In general, they dislike a transfer system that develops each year, pyjama cricket under floodlights, media hype, paparazzi-style invasions of players' private lives, Lillee-type intractability and reverse sweeps.

They much prefer the classical attainments of a Greg Chappell, the wiles of a Lindsay Hassett or Richie Benaud, the honest endeavour of an Alan Davidson and the pugnacious determination of an Allan Border. And even if these are all Australians, and English loyalties are temporarily subsumed, it does not really matter. After all, there is always Botham. With all his extravagances, who knows what he will do?

Most lovers of the game will never make the admission, but this simple vocation with bat and ball, whose genesis is obscured by the tippet of time, is their reason for living. Was it not Harold Pinter who said 'I tend to believe that cricket is the greatest thing that God ever created on Earth'?

An ivory M.C.C. life membership badge No. 1, engraved '*George Cecil Ives*'. In order to repay William Nicholson, who had advanced £18,000 to purchase the freehold of Lord's, the club elected 200 life members between 1888 and 1892. Each member subscribed £100.

A snooze at the seaside. Hove, 1979. The game that has receded into oblivion is between Sussex and Somerset.

# Bibliography

The following books and magazines have been used for reference in the preparation of this volume.

The list is not comprehensive; other sources and attributions are to be found within the text. Recourse has been made also to newspapers ancient and modern, and to annuals such as *Wisden's Almanack*.

Ashley-Cooper, *Cricket and Cricketers*, Philadelphia U.S.A., 1907.

Ashley-Cooper, *Some Notes on Early Cricket Abroad*, The Cricketer Magazine, 1922–23.

Buckley, *Fresh Light on 18th Century Cricket*, Cotterell & Co., Birmingham, 1935.

Buckley, *Historical Gleanings*, Lord's library MS, 1954.

Barty-King, *Quilt Winders and Pod Shavers*, Macdonald & James, London, 1979.

Bowen, *Cricket: A History of its Growth and Development throughout the World*, Eyre and Spottiswoode, London, 1970.

Frith, *Pageant of Cricket*, Macmillan, London, 1987.

Goulstone, *Early Kent Cricketers*, International Research Publications, 1971.

Goulstone, *The 1789 Tour*, International Research Publications, 1972.

Henderson, *Ball, Bat and Bishop*, Rockport Press Inc. New York, 1947.

Hone, *Cricket in Ireland*, The Kerryman Ltd., Tralee, Eire, 1953.

Labouchère, Provis and Hargreaves, *The Story of Continental Cricket*, Hutchinson, London, 1969.

Lewis, *Double Century*, Hodder and Stoughton, London, 1987.

Mandle, *Cricket and Australia Nationalism in the 19th Century*, Royal Australian Historical Society, Vol.59, 1973.

Mandle, *W.G. Grace as a Victorian hero*, Canberra College of Advanced Education, Australia

Mangan, *Athleticism in the Victorian and Edwardian Public School*, Cambridge University Press, 1981.

Martineau, *They Made Cricket*, Museum Press, London, 1956.

Methven Brownlee, *W.G. Grace, a biography*, Iliffe and Son, London, 1887.

Nyren/Cowden Clarke/Arlott, *The Young Cricketer's Tutor*, Davis-Poynter Ltd., London, 1974.

Parker, *The History of Cricket*, Seeley Service & Co., London, 1950.

Pollard, *The Formative Years of Australian Cricket*, 1803–93, Angus and Robertson, N.S.W., Australia, 1987.

Rait-Kerr, *The Laws of Cricket*, Longmans, Green & Co., London, 1950.

Sackville-West, *Knole and the Sackvilles*, Ernest Benn Ltd., London, 1922.

Simon & Smart, *Art of Cricket*, Martin Secker & Warburg Ltd., London, 1983.

*The Sportsman's Magazine*, Vols.1–3, Dipple, London, 1845–47.

Squire & Squire, *Henfield Cricket and its Sussex Cradle*, Sussex, 1949.

Swanton & Woodcock, *Barclays World of Cricket*, London, 1980.

Synge & Cooper, *Tales from Far Pavilions*, Pavilion Books, London, 1984.

Thomas (H. P-T.), *Old English Cricket*, Richards, Nottingham, 1923–29.

Waghorn, *The Dawn of Cricket*, Tomsett & Co., London, 1906.

In recent years, the standard red has been replaced by other hues for experiment, and as an aid to visibility for games in extraordinary conditions.

# Index

The vast leather-bound manuscript *Index to Scores and Biographies*,
of which three exist, compiled by Alfred Caston. The slim book
in red-ribbed morocco resting negligently on top is Norman Gale's
*Cricket Songs*. The ball is a Saxon souvenir from Lord's Cricket
Ground.